Presented To:

Phil Roberts

By:

COMMUNITY UMC,

Date:

_9/10/06_

apples & chalkdust #2

by
Vicki Caruana

RIVER
OAK
PUBLISHING

Tulsa, Oklahoma

2nd Printing

apples & chalkdust #2:
More Inspirational Stories and Encouragement for Teachers
1-58919-811-5
Copyright © 2001 by Vicki Caruana

Published by RiverOak Publishing
P. O. Box 700143
Tulsa, Oklahoma 74170-0143

Dedicated to Fred

Introduction

News is made and presidents are elected on educational issues. School vouchers, standardized testing, and the grading of schools flash across headlines and television screens. But teachers know that the real issues, the ones that matter on a daily basis, are far more numerous and much deeper. For some reason, teachers—whether in large urban high schools or small rural elementary schools—face their daily issues alone, rarely reaching out for help, even from those who understand the most. Requesting help is often seen as a weakness. Yet, how can we help the students in our charge if we can't even help each other?

I've received hundreds of e-mails from teachers all over the world praising me for *Apples & Chalkdust* and seeking advice. These teachers, looking for a reason to stay in the profession, feel helpless and alone. Although I'm honored to lend a listening ear and encouraging words, it breaks my heart that teachers feel like their only hope is to e-mail a stranger far away. Inside each of our schools are people with hearts just like yours. Look around and seek out like-minded colleagues. Support one another. Give to others what you seek for yourself—acceptance, encouragement, and honor.

I pray that this edition of *Apples & Chalkdust* ministers to you and leads you to lend a hand to others. All we have to do is let the world know what the real issues are and do the best job we can. Most of all, we must remember that it's not about us at all—it's about the children.

Vicki Caruana

"Everyone who remembers his own educational experience remembers teachers, not methods and techniques. The teacher is the kingpin of the educational experience."
—Sidney Hook

Celebrate!

Helen felt uncomfortable in a restaurant alone. Since her husband's death, she had avoided going out alone. But today was special. It was their anniversary, and she wanted to celebrate it the way they always had. Her silent reminiscing was threatened by an unusually large group of teenagers. They were celebrating something as well, but they were much too loud about it. And since her retirement from teaching, she just didn't have the tolerance for noisiness anymore.

Helen tried to block out their conversations and bursts of laughter, but it was impossible. She hadn't ordered yet, so she decided to just leave. As she reached for her purse, she heard one slice of their conversation that made her sit back down and unassumingly eavesdrop.

"Can you believe it? We made it! Graduated!" one girl, all in black, said.

"I wouldn't have . . . except for Mr. Baldwin," said another. "I'll never forget him."

"What did he do?"

"He didn't give up on me. Even when I wanted him to," she said. "I'll miss him."

Helen Baldwin's eyes brimmed with tears. They were talking about Frank, her Frank! He was their favorite teacher.

"May I join you?" Helen asked the table of celebrators. "Frank Baldwin was my favorite as well."

Teach today to be the favorite teacher remembered tomorrow.

"Superior teachers make the poor students good and the good students superior."
—Marva Collins

Let It Shine!

Dan clutched his principal's permission to start a young writers' club securely in his hand. It was a new day! Finally a chance to make a difference outside the traditions of the classroom. Finally a way into the hearts of more than just his own students.

The first day of club was overwhelming. Sixty fifth graders showed up and squeezed into Dan's smaller-than-average classroom. The fifth grade teachers showed up as well, most out of curiosity, but some hoping Dan would fail.

"What's Jason doing here?" one teacher exclaimed in an indignant whisper. "I can't even get him to write a complete sentence."

"Look who else is here," another pointed out. "Jessica couldn't spell even if her life depended on it."

The gaggle of teachers laughed loudly, interrupting Dan's opening remarks to his students whose eyes were glued on him as if waiting to finally hear a well-kept secret. His gaze in their direction finally caused the group to leave—all but one.

After three weeks of club, students were asked to share from their writing journals something they were particularly proud of. Jason rose to his feet and began to read. After five emotionally charged pages, his teacher, the one who had remained, was in tears. "I never expected . . ." she tried to say.

"I always knew . . ." Dan said, putting an arm around her shoulders.

Give students a measure of grace, and you will see how much you make a difference.

"The man [or woman] who can make
hard things easy is the educator."
—Ralph Waldo Emerson

The Tutor

Angie Becker soothingly stroked her expanding belly as she watched Jonathon struggle through the algebra problem on the board. She had committed to work with him after school each day for this marking period. It seemed like the only way to give him the extra attention and time he needed to bring up his failing grade. Angie's pregnancy may have tired her physically, but she never tired of the satisfaction and utter joy she felt when Jonathon finally grasped a concept.

Teaching one-on-one in a tutorial way brings two people closer together. Angie felt both pride and affection for this student. He had become close to her as well. But one day, five weeks into their time together, Angie doubled over in pain. In what felt like a frenzy of activity, Angie was whisked away from the school in an ambulance. The last thing she saw was Jonathon's concerned face as he stood helplessly at his desk.

Three weeks later, after the end of the marking period and a less than effective substitute, Angie returned to school. She eyed the pile of work to be graded, and her heart fell as she realized it was too late for Jonathon. As she sifted through that pile, she came upon a plain white envelope. Inside was a card, and on it was scribbled in Jonathon's less than perfect handwriting, "I'm sorry you lost your daughter. But please know you did real well with a son. I got a B! Thank you."

Take the time to make someone else's day a little easier.

"Teaching should be such that what
is offered is perceived as a valuable
gift and not as a hard duty."
—Albert Einstein

Starting School Too Soon

Danice made the decision to go back to teaching
when her son began kindergarten. It was the ideal
situation. They would be at the same school! That
way she could keep an eye on him and see how he
adjusted to school those first few weeks. She had
held him back a year because he was a summer baby
and she didn't feel he was ready. Now, if there were
any problems, she'd be right there. It would be just
as she'd always dreamed it would be. Picture perfect!

And it was perfect, for a while. Christopher settled
into kindergarten more easily than Danice settled into

working full-time again. He acted as if he'd always been there; she felt as if she'd never been there! What was wrong with her? Her signed year contract was the only thing that kept her from resigning.

As it turned out, it was Danice who had gone back to school too soon, not her son. Mounting pressures at home and school made this long-awaited experience a dreadful, unfulfilling one. She admitted to her husband that she had made a mistake, and together they planned for her to stay home once again the next year. It would take careful planning because financially it seemed inadvisable.

Now with the knowledge that she could correct her mistake, Danice was free to give herself to her job and her students. Even though she knew she'd leave them at the end of the year, she also knew that while she was there, they deserved her best.

Give your best, even when you feel your worst.

"The greatest sign of success for a teacher
. . . is to be able to say, 'The children
are now working as if I did not exist.'"
—Maria Montessori

Planned Obsolescence

Michele teaches gifted students at an elementary school in New Mexico. She loves teaching, and it shows. Her high energy is due to a desire to witness and possibly be a part of student learning. She has one great concern. Her students' passion to learn extends only to her own time with them. As complimentary as that may seem, Michele wants more for them.

Her goal? To work herself right out of a job! Her dream? That all of her students, and others like them, can have their needs served right in their regular classrooms. She knows that the state's inclusion program could be put into effect at her school and wants her students to be prepared.

Michele has decided to give her students the tools they will need to succeed, no matter what their learning environment may be. After all, it's not about her; it's about them! Their success will be measured by their adaptability and desire to learn even without her. Just as parents measure the success of their lessons by how their children behave when they are not around, teachers must look for those same results. "I'll be happy when they don't need me anymore—when they can take what's thrown at them and run with it!" Is this really possible? Her heart is right, and time will tell.

> You have a telltale heart; it lets everyone know by your actions whose needs you put first.

"There is something that is much more
scarce, something rarer than ability.
It is the ability to recognize ability."
—Robert Half

Diamond in the Rough

Susan began straightening the chairs as the last
fifth grader left her Sunday school classroom.
Looking up she saw Mark at her door. Mark was
the youth pastor, and his face spoke of concern.

"How did Josh do today?" Mark inquired.

Susan lit up! "He prayed out loud for me
today," she said. "He didn't have to say anything,
but he chose to take the risk and prayed for me."

"Did he disrupt the class today?" Mark acted as
if he hadn't heard Susan.

"No. No more than anyone else," she said.

"Then he did cause trouble?"

"No! Didn't you hear me? He thought about someone else today besides himself. He prayed for someone."

She continued. "Josh knows more than we give him credit for. He gave answers I didn't expect and insights I hadn't seen. I thanked him privately for his answers. You know he doesn't like attention called to him."

"No, I didn't know that," Mark replied.

"I know him a little better now," Susan said. "It just takes time."

Upon leaving the room, Mark wondered why he hadn't noticed the things that Susan noticed about Josh. Was it really just a matter of taking the time?

Take the time to get to know your students by heart, not by reputation.

"It is a luxury to learn; but the luxury
of learning is not to be compared
with the luxury of teaching."
—Roswell Dwight Hitchcock

No Substitutions, Please!

Esther is a great school secretary. What she
accomplishes in a day rivals any corporate giant.
One task, however, is especially distressing to her.
When her phone rings at 6:00 A.M., even before she
has left for school, she knows it's a teacher calling
in sick. She sighs in disappointment, then answers
the phone as she prays that a suitable substitute
will be available today.

Why is this such a hassle? Esther knows it is
part of her job description. She doesn't dispute its

necessity. She just knows that today will now be messier than usual and will require her patience. The substitute, if she can find one in time (for they are a limited bunch), will arrive just in time to lead in the pledge. He will then scramble for the rest of the day playing catch-up.

More often than not, the day goes poorly for both the students and the stand-in teacher, and Esther will hear about it. She knows teachers are entitled to use their sick days. She also knows that the teacher's presence brings stability and peace. It's one of the only jobs that is so adversely affected by the absence of an employee. No guilt is intended when Esther greets the teacher with relief upon his return. He is, after all, the teacher—and she appreciates his presence.

Stay healthy— not just for yourself. Your absence affects a multitude!

"The gift of teaching is a peculiar
talent and implies a need and a
craving in the teacher himself."

—John Jay Chapman

Art or Skill?

Sometimes beginning teachers are made to feel
like beginning athletes. They realize quickly that
there is much importance placed on the *skill* of
teaching. Make eye contact, conduct a beginning
and ending review, circulate the classroom, give
enough "think time," and most importantly, use
specific praise statements! As Sarah looked over
her first evaluation, she felt like teaching was more
like a carefully practiced skill than an art.

In this age of accountability, even veteran
teachers are relying more on the mechanics of

teaching than the artful grace of teaching. After all, one mistake and your school's rating may fall. One false move and your reputation may crumble. Sarah was just beginning to understand the rules of the game. She wasn't sure she liked the rules, but she desperately wanted to play the game.

But even an artist must first learn the skills required of him. Michelangelo had to first learn how to mix pigments as an apprentice in Florence. The mastery of skill gives way to the release of captivating art. Sarah would eventually captivate her students. However, during this apprenticeship, her first year, she needed to learn how to mix her pigments skillfully.

> Welcome the refining of your skills; they will serve you well in your artful craft of teaching.

"The place you are in needs you today."
—Katharine Logan

You Are Where You Belong

John couldn't wait to tell his wife the news! He finally got the transfer of his dreams. What seemed like a long time coming was finally here. He would become the curriculum specialist at another school. The only down side was he wouldn't be teaching.

But as John bubbled on about how great this new job would be, he was the one who needed the convincing. "I know it's midyear, but you don't walk away from something like this," he explained. "I know I'll miss the kids, but this gives me a chance to affect many more children."

"When do they expect you to start?" his wife asked.

John knew inside that this was the sticky part. "They expect me in two weeks."

"Kids are resilient. They'll adapt. I'm sure whoever takes your place will care for them as you have."

I wonder, thought John.

The next two weeks were a blur. His students needed reassurance, but all he could do was pack boxes, complete overdue paperwork, and coach the new teacher about what to do and how to do it. This was not how he wanted to leave. It was, however, how he left.

Remember, you are where you are for a reason. That reason just happens to be about four feet tall with two incredulous eyes and lots of questions.

Don't walk away until you've met those eyes straight on.

Even in the midst of transition, don't forget the ones you are leaving behind.

> "A dull teacher, with no
> enthusiasm in his own subject,
> commits the unpardonable sin."
> —R. C. Wallace

What's Your Passion?

"Who was your favorite teacher, Diane?" Julie asked her friend as they watched their children play together on the beach.

"That's easy. Mr. Danker, my tenth grade Biology teacher. He was strange, that was for sure. But I still remember everything we did in his class. He was also into taxidermy, and above each of our desks hung some sort of stuffed animal!" Diane excitedly explained.

"Oh, how gross!" Julie was horrified.

"No, it was cool. Each week we had a test, and it was difficult. But we could improve that grade if we dared. We could gain extra credit if we ate, without gagging, something he brought in—like oysters, squid, or even pig's feet!" Diane was quite animated now.

"I remember that we created a huge animal collage all through the year. You could only put something on it if you could identify it and tell one defining characteristic. At the end of the year, part of our final exam was to find a particular animal on that collage, identify it, and remember that characteristic. You know, I haven't thought about that in years. Why don't our children's teachers teach like that?" Diane's joy ended abruptly.

Are we teaching like that? Can your students see your passion in what you teach?

If you don't have passion, find it! Only then can you light that same flame in your students.

"They know enough who
know how to learn."
—Henry Adams

Vertical Moves

What an incredible semester this had been! Jon had taken two classes at the university toward his degree in Educational Leadership—the principal track. His eyes were now open to realities he never knew existed as a teacher.

He discovered that public education is supposed to be free. Sounds like that is common knowledge, but you wouldn't know it in this climate of the technology race and the desire to provide high interest activities for students. Fundraising had become the unwritten goal of many schools, and Jon's was no exception. He was beginning to wonder about his school's focus.

Were the needs of the children driving their goal, or was it the need of the faculty not to be left behind? They had made up wish lists for parents, solicited from the business community, and started selling advertisements in the school newsletter—all to raise money to get things they believed were necessary to increase student achievement. But were they? Jon wasn't so sure anymore.

Education is costing more and more each year. Unfortunately, student achievement is not increasing at a parallel rate. If money is the answer to student achievement, then what do we say to those in poorer districts—that their children will never be able to succeed? When teachers teach—really teach—students learn. That is the variable most worth investing in.

> Creative teaching doesn't have to cost a fortune. Look for ways to use the resources available to you to enhance your teaching.

"Who dares to teach must
never cease to learn."
—John Cotton Dana

Creature Feature

Carol Dome's classroom was noisy, crowded,
and sometimes even smelled! But it wasn't her
students' fault—it was the animals. Carol believed
that elementary school is a time for exploration
and discovery. Creation was up close and personal
for her students, and they used any spare moment
to observe and comment on their surroundings.
The circle of life included them, and Carol's
teaching helped connect them all. All except her
principal, Mr. Dawsey.

All he saw upon entering her class was chaos.
He didn't even know where to begin to conduct her
teacher evaluation. He knew the students loved

this teacher; he just wasn't convinced much learning was going on. Until one day . . .

The children were unusually reticent and calm when Principal Dawsey entered that day. One of the baby chicks, newly hatched, had died suddenly. Carol Dome was sitting in their midst on the floor, her hands cupped around the now still chick. Each child quietly opened their journals and wrote their reactions to this event. Then one child moved to the bulletin board and adjusted the growth chart of their animal nursery. Finally, another child fetched their book on hatching chicks and read aloud the section about problems during hatching.

Mr. Dawsey saw these children apply a myriad of skills that day, even in the midst of tragedy. Carol Dome's evaluation was a much clearer task to him now. Learning was indeed occurring—even for him.

There is more than one right way to teach.

"I delight in learning so that I can teach."
—Seneca

The Great Adventure

Teachers, on the whole, are an underappreciated lot—until they choose to leave the classroom. Janis left. After sixteen years—ten of which she'd spent at the same school—she left the classroom in favor of a teacher training position.

Reaching as many children as possible, as deeply as possible, was both her professional and her personal goal. Her fulfillment was measured by her success in the classroom. Voted Teacher-of-the-Year two years before, she was at the top of her game. Parents begged for their children to be in her class. Those who weren't were usually desperately disappointed. That disappointment concerned Janis.

She thought there should not be one excellent teacher in a grade—or a school for that matter. There should be many. Janis decided she would encourage all the teachers at her school with newfound strategies and untapped insights she'd learned along the way. Reception of these ideas was usually mixed, but slowly teachers at her school began to look outside of themselves toward new horizons.

Janis, always seeking those new horizons, found a way to legitimately share them with hundreds of teachers in her new position. Appreciation for her talent climaxed on her last day. Amid the students' tears, you could see how deeply she had touched them. She had succeeded!

You may not know your successes or how much you are truly appreciated until you've moved on.

"Those having torches will
pass them on to others."
—Plato

Who Pays Your Dues?

Debbie's new teaching job was in a sixth
grade center in the housing projects of Tampa,
Florida. Not what she had pictured. Not what
she had hoped for. She taught severely learning
disabled students who went home each day to an
empty house, witnessing atrocities she only saw
briefly on the nightly news. How could she
compete with that?

Debbie fully expected to teach well, and she
expected her students to then learn. Her
expectations were both too high and flawed. She
ended up spending most of the year sparring with
them instead—once even physically! All of her

college training did not prepare her for this assignment. Only time and on-the-job experience could have done that.

Many beginning teachers in these situations believe they are just "paying their dues." But their inexperience does not foster student achievement.

When considering a new teaching assignment, it's okay to look for a challenge, but make sure you're not getting yourself in over your head. Remember that it will be your students who pay if you take on a challenge you're not able to rise to.

If you set yourself up for success, you'll also be paving the way for your students to succeed.

"The true aim of everyone who aspires
to be a teacher should be, not to impart
his own opinions, but to kindle minds."
—Frederick William Robertson

Bill Myers - Electrifying

Bill Myers' willingness to learn and be open
to new ideas has made him one of the most
electrifying teachers. As a prolific author and film
director, he is an obvious success. Less obvious,
but seemingly more important to him, is his
success as a teacher. From the Sunday school
classroom to a young writers' conference room, he
imparts knowledge as if he is giving a gift.

Each gift is carefully chosen, attractively
wrapped, and delivered with the anticipated
excitement of the recipient. The gift itself is

priceless advice from an expert craftsman. His generosity generates edge-of-their-seats enthusiasm in his students. Bill, who claims he himself has only about a five-minute attention span, can somehow hold the interest of thirty third- through fifth-graders for hours!

How does he do this? How can *you* do this? By loving what and who you teach so much that your students can't help but be mesmerized by you. Enthusiasm is contagious! And if enthusiasm leads to success, then ask yourself what your students are "catching" from you? If success breeds more success, how are you measuring yours? Bill Myers knows how to light a fire; he just touches his flame to his students' lives.

Is electricity in the air in your classroom? If not, check the power supply first.

"The word is half his that speaks,
and half his that hears it."
—Montaigne

Are You Listening?

by Helen Peterson

This was a steady day of testing for Sharon, a special education teacher. Staffings were near, and she needed to finish testing these students. She concentrated on keeping to her schedule in order to finish before the end of the day.

The last student she tested was Sean, a first grader who was struggling to learn.

He began answering the test questions very willingly, but as the session became longer and questions harder, he complained that this was "boring."

Sharon gave him a restroom break hoping that was the problem. But when he came back, he still assured her that this test was "too boring."

Finally, Sharon asked him what he thought the word, *boring,* meant.

"Too hard," he whispered.

Later, as she was writing her anecdotal summary of Sean's testing behavior, she was relieved that she decided to ask him that one question. His report now reflected a more accurate behavior than she had thought initially.

How often do we as teachers assume that we know what children are saying to us without asking the right questions? How often do our students assume they know what we are saying? How often are we both wrong?

In order for you and your students to be communicating with each other, you both need to be on the same page.

"Other people can't make you see with
their eyes. At best they can only
encourage you to use your own."
—Aldous Leonard Huxley

What You See Is What You Get

As Sarah paces the middle school lunchroom
during her lunch duty, she recalls her dad's words.
"Make the boss look good," Dad had said. "That's your
job." But today Sarah isn't so sure it is that simple. The
students are more out of control than usual, and Sarah
sees things with her eyes that she wouldn't dare utter
with her mouth. Yet she feels her hands are tied.
Report trouble or turn her eyes away? After all it's just
seventh graders being seventh graders.

It's more than the sliminess she feels under her feet or the elevated volume that's probably a hazard to her hearing. It's the cruelty, the utter disregard for personal space, and the humiliation she witnesses students suffering every day. This is not a safe place to be—not for her or for students.

After lunch Sarah invisibly strolls into the front office. Without even breaking her stride, she picks up an official behavior report form. Back in her classroom she fills in every detail she has witnessed over the past six weeks, then sits back to muster the courage to sign her name to it. It's time to take a stand. She knows it won't make the principal look good, but her conscience is screaming.

Sarah signs and delivers copies to the appropriate mailboxes. What comes next? She doesn't know. But she does know that silence means agreement.

Struggling with an ethical issue? Do the right thing. You're only accountable for your own actions.

"My heart is singing for joy this morning.
A miracle has happened! The light of
understanding has shone upon my little pupil's
mind, and behold, all things are changed."
—Anne Sullivan

The Ah-Ha Effect

Not covered in any college textbook is the
sensation of "Ah-ha!" when a student finally
understands what was once an incomprehensible
concept to him. Judy learned that firsthand when
she tutored a boy diagnosed with a math disability.
It wasn't her student's discovery that changed her,
however; it was her own.

She had learned how to break the learning of a
new concept back down to the concrete level if a
student was having trouble. So when it came to
fractions, a trip to the pizza parlor seemed in order.

Not just because it would be fun, but because Judy herself had always struggled with fractions. Teaching the lesson step-by-step (including consuming the prop) led Judy to an amazing discovery—she finally understood fractions! For the first time in her life, she really understood them! This made teaching them not only easier, but more exciting.

Should it have taken Judy until she was twenty to fully grasp fractions? Unknown. What is known to her now, however, is the power of the Ah-ha effect. She knows that it doesn't really matter how long it takes, as long as it happens. Maybe it will take a different approach. Maybe a student just needs more time. What are you willing to do to ensure your students' success? Your work is not done until you hear, "Oh, I get it!"

> Do you know which students "get it" and which don't? You should. Take the time and give more when needed.

"Unless one has taught . . . it is
hard to imagine the extent of the
demands made on a teacher's attention."
—Charles E. Silberman

Homework

"Come to bed," Joe called from the bedroom. Sally was still at the kitchen table, surrounded by a mound of papers that held her hostage.

"In a minute," a yawn garbled her answer and tempted her to bed. "I promised my kids I'd get these reports back to them by tomorrow."

"Don't you have time to do this at school?" Joe ignorantly asked.

Sally couldn't believe he could ask this. *How long have I been teaching? Ten years. Doesn't he know by now what this job entails? Obviously not.* Just then, a red flier underneath her piled reports caught her attention, "The Great American Teach-In." Suddenly Sally was wide awake with mischievous intent.

"Joe, can you come to my class next week for The Great American Teach-In and tell the kids all about your job?"

Joe agreed. He spent three hours with Sally's sixth graders. Sally enjoyed learning more about Joe's job, and Joe got to experience some of the joys and frustrations of teaching. During lunch he begged off, saying that he'd been called back to work. Sally smiled shyly as she watched her husband pull out of the faculty parking lot.

That night while again amidst her pile, Sally was content, knowing her husband had tasted teaching. She knew he understood now when he said, "I don't know how you do it, because I sure couldn't do that every day!"

Share the wealth! Invite your spouse to school. It will be an education for both of you.

"Educators should be chosen not merely
for their special qualifications, but more
for their personality and their character,
because we teach more by what we are
than by what we teach."

—Will Durant

Character Sketch

It was time again for textbook adoption. This
year the adoption committee was considering health
textbooks. Donna knew that a qualifying indicator for
adoption was whether or not character building was
included. Donna knew there was trouble when she
called the meeting to order and saw the three parents
who made up one-third of the adoption committee
sitting with their arms folded and lips pressed tight.

"None of these texts represent what I believe
my children should think," one mother said.

"I don't see any emphasis on right and wrong. Everything is so wishy washy," said another.

Donna knew she would have to keep her own beliefs to herself, address each concern, and solicit alternative solutions to the problem. Respectfully, she asked each member to write down what character traits they hoped children would learn in school and how that might best be accomplished.

The parents silently but reverently got down to business. Realizing that what they had to say mattered, the parents relaxed, and real work was accomplished. They did not adopt a new health curriculum, but chose instead to integrate timeless truths into every content area. The first line of defense, they agreed, was the teacher. Donna had already modeled that for them.

Character building begins in you, not in a textbook.

"I was still learning when
I taught my last class."
—Claude M. Fuess

Amy Has Left the Building

The day finally arrived. Amy looked around the classroom she used to call her own. Just the box containing the contents of her desk remained. Her last day of teaching—a bittersweet day. Amy soothed her ever growing belly and wondered if this little one would ever understand what she gave up to be with him.

It was as if she were walking through a fog as she locked her room for the last time. Jim, the custodian and one of her best allies, took the box from her and led her down the hallway.

"How about one last turn at hall duty?" he joked.

Amy stood at the entrance of the library and closed her eyes listening for the voices of the sea of sixth graders that filed through that same door each day. But now it was quiet, yet not completely silent. Amy walked through the double doors and into the welcoming arms and voices of her colleagues.

"Congratulations on the beginning of the rest of your life!" The shower surprised her.

At that moment Amy knew that even though she was leaving teaching, teaching would never leave her. Once a teacher always a teacher. Only now she would have the distinct privilege of having a classroom of one.

Even if your days in the classroom are over, your days as a teacher will never end.

"What a teacher thinks she teaches often has little to do with what students learn."

—Susan Ohanian

Just Julie

Julie loved teaching preschool, and the fact that her students were special needs children only made her job more enjoyable. She felt like she was an intimate part of their lives.

Upon meeting parents, she always insisted that they call her by her first name. At only twenty-two, she hated being called Miss Julie—or even worse, Miss Haler. Even her students called her by her first name. She wanted them to think of her as their trusted friend, not just their teacher.

As the year progressed, Julie grew more and more weary of the daily lessons on living. Many of her students were not potty trained, even at four.

But it really wasn't the fact that she had to change diapers that bothered her. It was their unresponsiveness to her attempts to control their outbursts that puzzled Julie and left her exhausted. Sometimes parents volunteered in her class, and on those days the children seemed easier to train.

On one particularly patience-trying day, Julie excused herself to go to her office and regain her composure. What was she doing wrong? Even though she had a parent volunteer, not one student was obeying her. Just as she reentered the classroom, she overheard a parent reprimanding her own daughter, who had been unusually tempestuous that day.

"Alexandra, I expect you to listen to your teacher!" Mom said sternly.

"Why Mom? It's *just* Julie," Alexandra said, leaving Julie in shock—yet with her answer.

Finding it difficult to maintain control? Check to make sure you're still the teacher.

"I am teaching. . . . It's kind of like
having a love affair with a rhinoceros."
—Anne Sexton

Kid in a Candy Store

Linda couldn't wait to show her husband the exhibit hall at the convention. For five years she had attended alone, but this time they could afford to go together. Going into the exhibit hall was Linda's favorite part. She was like a kid in a candy store! Tim spent the whole day trotting after her and holding her various shopping bags.

"You've got to see this!" Linda dragged Tim to the elementary reading booth of a well-known curriculum vendor. "Can you believe it? Finally, a reading program that incorporates writing, but in a way that is relevant and high interest."

Tim just stared at her blankly as if she were speaking another language.

"Isn't this exciting?" Linda could barely contain herself.

Tim snapped out of his confused daze and said, "That's great, Hon. You ready to get something to eat?"

Linda realized, once again, that Tim just didn't get it. Even though she knew that he couldn't possibly understand, she always hoped that maybe this time, he would. She also knew that there was no sense being disappointed about it. What mattered was that she was still excited about teaching. And coming to a convention always reminded her of that all-important fact.

The passion to teach is a unique gift. Even if others don't always understand your enthusiasm, rest assured that they'll be pleased with its results.

"One of the reasons why mature people stop growing and learning, is that they become less and less willing to risk failure."

—John Gardner

Vouchers

by Tony Horning

The teachers at Victory Academy seem to have an enthusiasm and energy about them that visitors almost always notice. There appears to be no difference in this enthusiasm between the new teachers and the veterans, nor does there appear to be any difference in this energy Monday through Friday.

One day Jon Bauer, a visiting consultant, noticed this unique culture and sat with some of the teachers to see if they could help him understand this school-wide phenomenon. The teachers he interviewed on the subject were bursting to tell him all about it!

"It's because of our vouchers," a first grade teacher said.

"Vouchers?" asked the consultant.

"Yes, they're great! You see, our principal gives us a voucher at the start of each school year. The voucher is good for one major mistake per week and unlimited minor mistakes for the entire year. Next year we're creating vouchers for our students, so they can be freed up to try over and over again without fear."

Jon couldn't help but wonder to whom in his life he could offer a voucher. His job was to ensure private schools met accreditation requirements. He wasn't supposed to tolerate mistakes. Yet today he thought maybe instead of a citation, he might write out a voucher instead.

Only when it's okay to fail is it okay to keep on trying.

"If you're too busy to help those
around you succeed, you're too busy."
—Bob Moawad

Too Busy

Elaine's worktable was covered with handouts
for tonight's open house. She had some clear goals
for both her students and their parents this year.
Twenty piles of paper lay on the table waiting for
what would bring them all together—the stapler.
But where was the stapler?

Students, who just moments earlier were
working quietly, slowly began to leave their desks
and gather at a far corner of the room. Elaine only
noticed in the most academic of ways; for she was
totally preoccupied with the task at hand and the
elusive location of the stapler. Someone was in
need, but Elaine didn't know it.

Finally, Elaine regained her students' attention with a double clap, and all returned to their seats—all but Jason. There he remained curled up on the floor in the corner. As Elaine approached the boy, she noticed his own work lying in a crumbled heap on the floor beside him. Jason held back his tears defiantly as Elaine knelt beside him. "What's wrong?"

It all came tumbling out. "I was trying to put my report in order. I just can't do this right!" Jason surrendered.

"Why didn't you raise your hand?" Elaine asked.

"I did." he said.

It was then that Elaine realized what the more important task was for today—and it wasn't finding the stapler.

The teaching of children should not be sacrificed in favor of paperwork—ever!

"One of the best ways to demonstrate
God's love is to listen to people."
—Bruce Larson

Listen! Do You Want to Know a Secret?

by Tony Horning

James Horner, an elementary principal, has a note pad on his desk. On that pad are the names of different parents, teachers, and staff along with the estimated time he has spent with each one over the course of the past five years. Through these records he has been able to come up with a chart to help him plan his day.

May I see you for just a minute? (Takes about seventeen minutes)

Do you have a moment? (Takes at least twelve
minutes)

Got a second? (Takes twenty-one minutes)

May I ask you a quick question? (Takes
thirteen minutes)

I NEED to see you right now! (Takes thirty-five
minutes—if crying, add another fifteen
minutes)

I just stopped in to touch base with you (Takes
twenty minutes—if coffee, add another
fifteen minutes)

With only so many hours in a school day, James
knows how precious each minute can be. Of course
Mr. Horner will see everyone who comes by—those
who are laughing, those who
come in crying, and everyone
in between. After all, there is
no better way to really share
someone's burden or rejoice
with them than to be willing
to listen with your
heart, as well as
your ears.

> Listen as
> though you
> were going
> to be tested
> at the end.

"I have always felt that the true
textbook for the pupil is his teacher."
—Mohandas K. Gandhi

A Lesson in Character

"What beautiful books these are!" Sandy said
after opening the new shipment of character
education books their district had recently ordered.
"Publishers are getting really good at making
textbooks more attractive and user friendly. That's
partially why I liked this series."

"I can't wait to get started," her partner, Janice,
said. "These kids are so rowdy this year. We really
need to teach them about strong character."

Sandy and Janice sorted the books by grade
level and took their own copies to their classroom.
They numbered them and assigned one to each
student. The very next day, they began the first

lesson. They were so excited, they didn't even preview the lesson. They were convinced that this curriculum would make a difference.

The first lesson was on perseverance. However, it took a lot longer to complete than expected. In fact, they were unable to complete their math that day because of it. Frustrated, Sandy skipped to the end of the lesson and gave the students the test. They did poorly. After some discussion, both teachers decided this curriculum was just one more thing they had to fit into their day. "We'll find another way to change their attitudes," Janice conceded.

But they never did.

Want your students to stick to their tasks and finish what they start? Make sure your own perseverance shines through!

"Teachers who set and communicate high expectations to all their students obtain greater academic performance from those students than teachers who set low expectations."

—Research Finding, U.S. Department of Education

Raise the Bar

Chuck taught above average sections of middle school math for fifteen years. He knew what it took for students to be successful in his classroom and was proud of the job he'd done all those years. Then on the last day of school, the secretary asked him to turn in his teacher's manuals because he would be teaching the below average sections this next term.

Chuck laughed aloud as he frantically tried to decide whether or not Mrs. Johnson was joking. Something was terribly wrong. His students had all done quite well. Then why had he been demoted?

Chuck reluctantly handed his manuals to Mrs. Johnson and turned to leave. His principal caught him by the elbow. "Chuck, I'm glad you're up for the challenge. These kids need you. I want only the best for them."

Chuck wasn't sure whether to thank Mr. Cohen or turn in his resignation. Next year would be far from easy. He couldn't depend on his tried and true methods. He'd have to work harder than ever before to reach these kids. And then he realized the source of his resistance and the opportunity this change could give him.

"Thanks for the opportunity, Mr. Cohen. It was time to shake things up a bit. Don't want to get lazy!" Chuck grabbed his new manuals and began to wonder what he could do to create success in his class next year.

When it becomes too easy, it's time to raise the bar. If you're not challenged, you don't learn.

"Woe to him who teaches men
faster than they can learn."
—Will Durant

Follow Those Tracks

Jim Spade watched painfully as one of his
students stood facing the blackboard for more than
five minutes without even making a scribble on it.
Day after day, he wondered what she was even
doing in his class. She was obviously not up to
Algebra in the eighth grade. Finally, exasperated,
Jim said, "Sit down, Miss Downy. Let's give
someone else a chance." Jim knew his frustration
with this student showed even more than a little.
Yet she was in his class, and there was nothing he
could do about it. He decided he would not hold
up the rest of the class, who clearly belonged there,
for this one inept student.

Carolyn Kane read Jim's remarks in the file of this misplaced student. Her heart broke. Where had the mistake been made? She looked at her last year's test scores and found that the student had tested out easily for the advanced math. Yet she was failing Jim's class, and now she was absent at least once a week. It was time for a conference, but not with the parents.

Jim's tightly folded arms told Carolyn all she needed to know. Jim felt no obligation to this student. Her failure was a blemish to him, something better ignored than dealt with. Yet it seemed too late in the year to move the student to the average math class.

Two afternoons a week, Carolyn tutored this student. It was not in her job description. It wasn't her problem. But it was necessary.

Being willing to give a little extra to help meet a student's need is what makes a good teacher great.

"Please remember these two difficult
truths of teaching: (1) No matter how
much you do, you'll feel it's not enough.
(2) Just because you can only do a
little is no excuse to do nothing."
—Susan Ohanian

A Test of Fire?

Jane Froman returned to the classroom after a
brief, three-year hiatus. She was amazed at how
many things had changed in her absence. Upon her
return she was handed an oppressive pile of new
assessment policies and a schedule for the training
that was necessary to make sense of the pile. Jane
blinked in disbelief as she realized that school
reform had taken them further away from teaching
and students further away from real learning.

The new state writing test was a prime example. The state's goal for students on this test, as unrealistic as it was, was tied to their funding. Poor scores equaled a poor school. Jane knew the expectation was that her students needed to score better than the year before. *How?* She wondered, since they were an entirely new set of students?

Her diligence paid off, and Jane's fourth graders did score exceptionally well on the writing test. However, Jane agonized over the myriad of skills she never got around to teaching, since she spent most of her time teaching to the test. Jane wants more for her students. Following her heart will undoubtedly add to her work, but finding that balance is the key to successful teaching.

Teaching to the test should never preclude meeting students' learning needs. Can you do both successfully?

"You take people as far as they will go,
not as far as you would like them to go."
—Jeannette Rankin

The Gardener

Susan learned long ago that not every child will achieve on grade level. Teaching severely learning disabled middle-schoolers gave her a chance to take students far, just not as far as the state was hoping for. By the time students had gotten to her, that fourth grade reading level was probably as high as they were going to go. Instead of looking to see how high they scored on the standardized tests, Susan concentrated on individual skills and learning strategies. She knew they could improve, but she wasn't going to disappoint herself and her students by expecting more than they could give.

"Aren't you being defeatist?" her intern asked.

"Not at all," Susan said. "I've just learned that it doesn't matter how lovingly you plant a seed, nor does it matter how rich the soil is or how well it is watered and fed, some just grow as tall as we imagined they would."

"Doesn't that disappoint you?"

"It used to. But now I've learned to see the beauty of each one, no matter how tall it grows or how glorious it blossoms," Susan said. She knew her intern didn't understand this flowery talk. Those who don't achieve as we hope are not weeds to be plucked out so the garden looks perfect. If you've ever tried to transplant a weed, you know that it doesn't survive. It grows stronger if allowed to stay right where it is.

> Set your students up for success by setting realistic expectations for them.

"America's future will be determined by the home and the school. The child becomes largely what it is taught, hence we must watch what we teach it, how we live before it."

—Jane Addams

Abraham Lincoln

Abe Lincoln got his education "by littles." His formal schooling only amounted to about one year. When he did attend school, it was in the backwoods of Indiana and Kentucky. In a poor school in those woods, no one would notice that his pants were too short, or that he had no shoes. Even though his own father mocked his attempts to get an education, Abe pursued learning regardless of what anyone else thought.

Hard work in rural Indiana in the early 1800's was defined as manual labor, not learning "readin', writin', and cipherin'." Abe was deemed lazy by most in his community. But Abe's stepmother encouraged his learning and made sure he always had a book in his hand. Sometimes it only takes one person to take an interest in a child for him to succeed.

Abraham Lincoln pursued knowledge and truth to the end of becoming President of the United States during our country's most turbulent period. Who would have thought that a gangly boy from the backwoods with almost no formal schooling would become one of our wisest leaders?

Look in your classroom today. You know that boy who comes to school in dirty clothes and is on free lunch? He may have exactly what it takes to make it in this world. You can choose to be his naysayer or his champion.

Some of our students may not look like winners on the outside. So take the time to find out who's on the inside.

"No one should teach who is
not in love with teaching."
—Margaret E. Sangster

Personal Image

This was her first faculty meeting! Amy
scanned the room for a familiar face and found
none. She felt more like it was her first day of
school. Everyone else settled into their seats as if
they owned them. Familiar cliques reunited after a
long, restful summer. "Just think," Amy said to
herself. "We're all here for the same reason. We
have the same mission."

Amy couldn't help but eavesdrop on the
conversations going on in front of and behind
her. She knew everyone must be as excited as she
was to welcome the children—their children.
Amy was wrong.

"Can you believe it?" someone said behind her. "They moved all my stuff just to paint the room! They didn't even have the decency to put it back the way I had left it!"

Then in front of her, "Look at her! She thinks just because she's a dean that she has power over us. It was only a few months ago that she was just a teacher like us."

And then right next to her, "You've got to be kidding! Look at my roster. More than five students in special education. What do they expect me to do? Work miracles?"

Where was the love of teaching? Where was the humility in knowing you would shape young minds? Amy looked in her pocket mirror for the answer. "I hope I never forget why I'm here," she whispered to the image.

When you can't remember why you're where you are, look in the mirror and ask the one who still remembers.

"A child educated only at school
is an uneducated child."
—George Santayana

Whose Side Are You On?

As Karan pens the last page of her book showing parents how to be partners in their child's education, it occurs to her how much times have changed. As a former teacher she understands how important it is for parents to be involved. But she has to smile as she remembers that her own mother never even attended parent/teacher conferences and rarely went to an open house night. All five of her children graduated from high school and college successfully. What has changed?

Karan's passion for education drives her to do whatever it takes to improve the lives of children in and out of her care. She goes above and beyond the call of duty in most cases. That is the message she presents to parents as well. Their influence supercedes her own as a teacher. Their input creates a longer lasting impact.

Maybe times will change again. Maybe someday it will be enough to just drop your child off at school and know that everything will go well. Maybe. But for now, a teacher's job doesn't end when the bell rings. It ends only when those in her charge learn. And at this time, that means forming strong partnerships with parents—being each other's lieutenant! This way you can do battle together!

Not sure where a parent's place is in the education process? Right at your side.

"Nothing fruitful ever comes when plants
are forced to flower in the wrong season."
—Bette Bao Lord

Say It Isn't So!

The caller's question made Junetta sigh. So often
when she did these radio shows, parents would call
in with questions that made her look like a hero.
But this question always made Junetta nervous. She
knew her answer could make parents angry with
her. Yet she couldn't avoid the truth. It would be
wrong for her to reinforce wrong thinking.

"My son's teacher wants to hold him back in
second grade, but I think she's wrong. How can I
convince the principal that the teacher is wrong?"

Junetta chose her words carefully but then said
them with confidence. "The truth is that principals
discourage teachers from recommending retention.

It doesn't look good on a school's record that they have retentions. But if this principal is standing behind his teacher's decision, I would take heed. She wouldn't made this recommendation unless she was sure."

"But his sister did so well at this school. He can too if we just move forward," the caller sounded desperate.

"I understand your concern, but I am more concerned about your son's future. Just because his sister did well in this school doesn't mean he will. What works with one does not work with another. Instead of forcing him into something before he's ready, why don't you give him the gift of time?" Junetta waited through silence for the caller's reply.

"I never looked at it that way, thank you."

Communicating the truth to someone without alienating them is a difficult job, but the truth will prevail.

"Little seedlings never flourish in the
soil they have been given, be it ever so
excellent, if they are continually pulled
up to see if the roots are grateful yet."

—Bertha Damon

A Matter of Time

The newspaper outlined the governor's
educational reform program all the way down to
what kindergartners should learn by the sixth month
of school! Jean sighed and threw the paper aside.
Some of the proposed changes sounded wonderful,
and the fact that the state actually intended to fund
them was unprecedented. Parents were encouraged,
and the governor was being hailed as a man ahead
of his time. But that was the problem—time.

Three years. The state gave the districts three
years to show leaps of progress. And if they didn't,

they would be shut down! As the elementary supervisor in her district, Jean knew all too well what would follow. She would do everything in her power to initiate the proposed reform. She would in-service her teachers, organize the orders for new materials, and then monitor the students' progress with standardized test scores. After twenty years in this position, she'd gone through these motions at least five times.

Yet things didn't change. In fact they got worse. The students, like young seedlings, may have been nurtured by expert gardeners and grown in the most beautiful garden, but they weren't being fed in the proper doses at the proper times. Most of these new ideas would work, and for some work miracles, yet the state expected results too fast.

Your methods are like slow-release fertilizers; over time they will produce a bountiful harvest.

"It is a mystery why adults expect perfection from children. Few grownups can get through a whole day without making a mistake."

—Marcelene Cox

Who Do You Owe?

Stan was in shock after his annual evaluation. There were too many check marks in the "Needs Improvement" column. Since he was on annual contract, he knew that if things didn't improve, the school was under no obligation to rehire him. Stan waited for the principal to remark on his failings.

The principal knew this had been a difficult year for Stan. The premature death of his wife had left him both numb and overwhelmed with the responsibilities of their three children. What Stan really needed today was support, not ultimatums.

"I know you must feel overwhelmed right now, Stan. I'm personally going to work alongside you to make up your work. In fact, I'll do much of it myself," the principal said.

Stan was so relieved by his principal's kindness. He returned to class with a new lease on life. As his students filed in, he checked the grade book for missing assignments. "Justin!" he shouted across the room. "Looks like you owe me two assignments. I expect them by the end of the day, or I'll drop you one letter grade."

As the student paled and panic swept his face, Stan remembered his own panic about his evaluation and the grace that was extended to him. He called Justin to his desk and said, "On second thought, why don't you come by after your last class and we'll work on those missing assignments together."

In need of grace? Don't forget to extend it to someone else as well.

"School is the marketplace
of possibility, not efficiency."
—Susan Ohanian

Defensive End

Denise couldn't believe she was involved in this kind of conversation once again. *Outsiders have no clue as to why schools make the decisions they make,* she thought. Although even as an insider, Denise didn't know why they made the decisions they made. Regardless, it was time once again to defend the public school system to her friends.

"What I don't understand is why they use a math program that clearly doesn't reach that many children."

"I want to know why there aren't enough textbooks, so my daughter can bring one home to do her homework."

The problem was that Denise had no answers for these questions. She knew that districts made decisions that made no sense to her or to any other teacher. She also knew that she and many others like her had dedicated their lives to public education because they believed they could make a difference in their students' lives.

She answered with confidence, "It's true that there are plenty of problems with the system, but let me tell you why I think the time I give to public education is important." Denise then shared with her friends her passion for teaching and some experiences from her classroom which kept her believing that she was touching lives and that learning was happening, even with the system's imperfections.

The best asset of any school is its dedicated teachers. When people complain to you about what your school doesn't have, gently remind them of what, and who, it does have to offer.

"Light tomorrow with today!"
—Elizabeth Barrett Browning

A Time to Plan
by Helen Peterson

"Congratulations on your retirement," Trevor, a first-year teacher, told Jim. "We are at opposite ends of this career, aren't we?"

"Not entirely. Retirement sneaks up on you very quickly. Have you begun to plan for your retirement yet?"

That question seemed odd to ask such a young teacher. Trevor asked him to elaborate.

"There's so much to consider, it's a shame to wait until the end," Jim began. "First, if you decide to teach in another town or district in state, please consider keeping your retirement plan intact. It's so expensive to buy those years back. And have you considered a savings plan yet?"

"Yes, I started one just this year," Trevor answered proudly.

"Good for you!" Jim told him sincerely. "Another important consideration, then, is this: keep interested in life. Don't let your career engulf all your time. Take time to develop deep relationships and explore hobbies and fitness sports. I read somewhere that you carry into retirement the interests you have nurtured all your life. So you see, you've got to get busy right now. Go for it! By the way, have you signed my book yet, *Oh, the Places You'll Go!*, by Dr. Seuss?"

As Trevor munched on a piece of Jim's retirement cake, he vowed to follow this sage advice.

Remember, it's never too early to prepare to retire.

Make lesson plans for your students and life plans for yourself.

> "If you promise not to believe everything your child says happens at this school, I'll promise not to believe everything he says happens at home."
>
> —Anonymous

He Said, She Said

"My dad says I don't have to listen to you!"

"You can't make me!"

"You want me to do what?"

Day after day, Sandy's ears stung with the words of her seventh graders. She was beginning to wonder what went on in the homes of these students. No wonder kids didn't respect their teachers. It sure sounded as if their parents didn't have any respect for them in the first place. One child in particular, David, shot remarks at Sandy almost daily. A conference was set with his dad for the next day. Sandy cringed at the thought of what she'd hear from this man as well.

A sullen Mr. Rankin slipped quietly into the student desk. Sandy had positioned it so that she could look down at him from her own desk during the conference. Both began the discussion with hesitancy.

"Mr. Rankin, your son is very bright. So much so that it surprises me you've told him he doesn't have to do anything he doesn't want to do," Sandy said.

"That's not how I heard it," Mr. Rankin said. "David says you refuse to help him when he doesn't understand his work."

"Obviously someone is missing from this conference," Sandy laughed.

"I can take care of that," Mr. Rankin said, opening the classroom door.

"Won't you join us, David?"

Make sure all parties are involved in a conference.

"A problem adequately stated is a
problem well on its way to being solved."
—R. Buckminster Fuller

Problem Solvers

Nancy's sixth-grade class buzzed with
excitement as they worked on their semester
project: Find a problem within the school and
generate solutions and a plan of action to solve it.
Nancy had taken a creative problem-solving class
during her master's studies and was anxious to try
out the technique with her own students. But the
first few days of the process turned into one gripe
session after another.

"We don't feel like we belong."

"We don't have a student council."

"The eighth graders pick on us in the halls."

On and on it went, one complaint after another. It was a mess, and Nancy needed to help her students focus on what the real problem was before they could ever consider trying to solve it.

"Let's try to formulate a problem this way: In what way(s) might we _____?" The students then listed all the problems they could think of in this way. After looking at the problems stated on the board, Nancy asked her students if they could think of one problem that narrowed the mess down. They did.

"In what way(s) might we build a sense of community in our school?" Reverent silence followed the realization that they had actually adequately stated the real problem. That was the hard part. Now brainstorming solutions wouldn't be so hard. They were focused and ready for action.

The first step to solving a problem is to be able to state it in a concise way.

"Education is a matter of building bridges."
—Ralph Ellison

There's No Place Like Home

(Written especially for the education
students at Keuka College, New York)

Cassie's decision to teach in her hometown
school was an easy one. She knew exactly where
she belonged. Yet upon applying, there were no
positions available. As a first-year teacher she
wanted to be surrounded by family and friends.

Cassie resisted suggestions to apply in the
city. But as fall approached and her dreams began
to fade, she decided to apply at a few schools in
the city.

Within days she had her first interview. She drove the thirty miles into the city and circled the building for fifteen minutes looking for a place to park. The building was old and musty and right in the middle of the wrong part of town. Cassie cringed at the thought of working there.

At the conclusion of her interview, she was offered the position. Exactly what she wanted, in the grade she wanted, but in the wrong place. The principal sensed her hesitation and offered to give her a tour.

"This would be your classroom," the principal said, waving his hand around the brightly lit room. "We're trying to create a friendly environment here. These kids are bussed in away from their neighborhoods and don't feel like they belong. We're trying our best to make them feel at home." At that moment,

Cassie realized that she was right where she belonged.

Keep your focus on your students, and you'll never get lost, even if you're far from home.

"There is no influence so powerful
as that of the mother, but next in rank
of efficacy is that of the schoolmaster."
—Sarah Josepha Hale

The Power of Love

Claire walked through the crowded hallway as if in a fog. She was only remotely aware of her son's tiny hand in hers as they approached his kindergarten classroom. The sights, the smells, and the sounds transported Claire back all those years ago to the day her own mother walked her to kindergarten. Where had the years gone? Everyone said that they grow up so fast. And everyone was right. Here was her little man all ready for school. It was a milestone, a day of ceremony and celebration.

Miss Sauri recognized the look on this mother's face even before she was inside the room. This was a face of a good mother, one whose love for her child showed from top to bottom. The trust between mother and son was communicated in a glance. Mom hung up his backpack and then knelt to give him instructions. Her son nodded in complete understanding and then turned to look at Miss Sauri with those same trusting eyes. *Mom has done a good job,* Miss Sauri thought.

Then Claire led her son to his teacher. Taking his hand and placing it in hers, she said, "He's all yours."

"No," Miss Sauri said. "He's yours. He's just on loan to me for now."

Never under-estimate the power of a mother's love. It's that love that will hopefully be transferred to you.

"Education has for its object the formation of character. This is the aim of both parent and teacher."

—Herbert Spencer

Me? A Teacher?

Chad wondered what his friends would think. He knew that his new job not only would surprise them; it would incite laughter! Chad, a teacher? No way! He never really liked school. He struggled more than some. But after years in a job he didn't train for or like, he knew he needed to change. Becoming a teacher was not his first choice, but it wasn't far-fetched either.

Chad's famed soccer career came to a crashing end when he wrenched his knee. Yet now with surgery, it was stronger than ever. His degree in science and a love for coaching was all he needed to convince himself that teaching in a high school might be a way to satisfy both loves. Midway through his teacher training, he received a job offer in a prestigious high school.

"What are your goals for your students?" the principal asked during his interview.

"I know this will sound idealistic, but I want them to love science. I want them, for maybe the first time, to see their connection to this place we call home. I want them to leave my class intent on making it a better place to live," Chad paused. "And I want to be for them what every patient teacher was for me—hope."

Chad knew it sounded like a reelection speech, but he couldn't help it. He meant every word. For the first time, he felt he was right where he belonged.

Those who can, teach. Those who wish they could only complain.

"If there is anything that we wish to change
in the child, we should first examine it
and see whether it is not something that
could better be changed in ourselves."

—Carl Jung

On My Honor

Steve cringed when he read the duty roster. In addition to his regular hall duty between classes, he also had to monitor the entire seventh-grade hallway during his free period.

"Just great!" Steve murmured. He knew that most teachers didn't bother to stand outside their doors between classes. He also knew that he was on his own if there was trouble. It would take a fire in the building to get some teachers away from their desks.

Steve watched the corridor for signs of unrest, but only minor infractions cropped up.

"Walk!"

"Get to class!"

"Ladies, this is not a beauty parlor."

Everyday reprimands.

Then suddenly, the hall exploded with voices. Steve made his way quickly toward the far end of the hall. There were eight classrooms in close proximity, but each door was closed to the turmoil in the hallway.

A girl's body was shaking violently on the hard tile floor. Her seizure frightened some and amused others, yet no one moved to help. Steve threw open the nearest door and slammed the call button. A teacher still at her desk looked bewildered. "Student down! Get help now!" Steve barked.

Your sense of duty to your students doesn't end inside the walls of your classroom. Duty is where duty calls.

"Teachers believe they have a gift for giving:
it drives them with the same irrepressible
drive that drives others to create a work
of art or a market or a building."
—A. Bartlett Giamatti

What He Left Behind

Freshman English was a huge class, and seventeen-year-old Jerry Jenkins cringed at the prospect of it. Already he knew that many professors expected students to figure it out for themselves. The fifty-minute classes were drudgery to get through. But Dr. Glenn Arnold was different.

From day one Jerry noticed an enthusiasm and commitment in this professor. The man actually enjoyed what he taught and paid more than just polite tolerance to his students. Dr. Arnold showed personal interest in all of them. He was completely prepared for each class and made what is usually just a requirement the highlight of Jerry's college experience. The class was a living testimony to his commitment. And it was catching!

Years later when Jerry's first book was published, he dedicated it to Dr. Arnold, a teacher whose influence reached into classes Jerry himself taught. He found out all those years later the secret to Dr. Arnold's success.

"My wife prayed for me every moment I taught," Arnold shared.

The circle of commitment was now complete. Mrs. Arnold was committed to her husband. Dr. Arnold was committed to his call. And his student Jerry Jenkins, through his commitment to the truth, was able to give back to his teacher the good things he had reaped as a result of both Dr. and Mrs. Arnold's commitment.

> Your commitment does not go unnoticed. It will return to you someday.

"The function of education is to teach one to think intensively and to think critically. Intelligence plus character—that is the goal of true education."

—Martin Luther King Jr.

Why?

"*Learn Critical Thinking Skills in 100 Easy Lessons?*" Sammie asked. "What kind of book is this?"

"The one from our Critical Thinking Skills workshop, remember?" Judy said with a yawn.

"Even if they are *easy* lessons, I don't have time to teach one hundred of them, do you?" Sammie knew she sounded negative, but she was tired of being told what to teach and how.

"Did anyone think *critically* about including this in our daily lessons?"

"Doubt it," Judy said.

"I have an idea. Let's figure out a way to encourage critical thinking without using this book," Sammie suggested.

"You don't need to tell me," Judy explained. "I've always taught my students to think about why they do what they do, and how to use what they learn in their everyday lives. It's a matter of attitude."

Sammie realized that Judy didn't need this textbook. But at the same time, she knew that she did. "How can I have that attitude?" Sammie questioned.

Judy could see that Sammie was serious now. Concern was written all over her face. "You already do, just by asking the question 'why.' The key is to encourage your students to do the same."

To think critically is not being critical—it's being smart.

"All our children deserve teachers
who believe they can learn and who
will not be satisfied until they do."
—Joe Nathan

Together Forever

Shelly was frantic. Two of her sixth graders
were still failing, even after numerous attempts on
her part to bring them up to speed. Only six weeks
remained until their fate would be determined.

She had tried after-school tutoring, peer tutoring,
and adjusting her teaching methods. These two
students were completely different economically,
ethnically, intellectually, and personally. They only
had one thing in common—their parents' apparent
lack of involvement in their education.

Finally Shelly met with each boy, hoping to gain some insight into his learning styles and motivation.

All Shelly got out of the first student was, "I don't know." Discouraged and still no closer to a solution, she met with the second student.

"Is Jason going to fail? Will he have to go to summer school? If I fail, can we go to the same summer school?" The student flung question after question at Shelly. Then it hit her!

"Michael, are you failing on purpose so you can stay with Jason?"

Michael hesitated but then said, "Someone has to. He's my friend, and now that his dad is out of work, he only feels safe with me."

It explained everything.

"Okay Michael, let's work on this together. How about instead of you both failing together, you succeed together?"

Dig a little deeper and, if you still come up empty, go back and dig deeper still.

> "Servant of All is a greater title
> than King of Kings."
> —F. Crane

VIP

by Tony Horning

They saw him on the school grounds, walking around and looking at the ground as if he'd lost something. Later in the day, they saw him picking up trash around the playground. During recess, they saw him pulling weeds from the flower beds in the front of the school. He was dressed much nicer than a custodian. He wasn't a teacher. Who was this man?

Mrs. Nader's kindergarten class was just beginning to get to know their school, its teachers, and its staff. They'd met Mrs. Ludy, the lunch lady, because she served them every day. They knew Mr.

Foster, the custodian, because he fixed their sink one day. And they knew Miss Dansen, the secretary, because they delivered the attendance to her each day. By the end of the first week, they knew all the important people.

Then on Friday, the man they saw picking up trash and weeding the garden came into their class. He brought their teacher a bouquet of flowers and said, "Kids, you have one of the best teachers in the whole world. I hope you enjoyed your first week of school."

"Who is that man, Mrs. Nader?"

Mrs. Nader chuckled. "That's Mr. Clark, our principal. He cares a lot about our school and wants to keep it looking as nice as possible."

"He sure works hard."

"Yes, he does," she said.

If you think you're a servant, check your reaction the next time you're treated like one.

"There is more treasure in books than in
all the pirate's loot on Treasure Island."
—Walt Disney

Never Judge a Book
By Its Cover

Joan had gone to great lengths to educate her
faculty about the nature and needs of gifted
students. Yet every year there was at least one
teacher who suffered from elective ignorance.
Simply put, the teacher wanted things her way,
even at the expense of her students.

Chris was leap years ahead of every other second
grader. His parents, after numerous conferences, just
told their son to comply even if he already knew the
material. But it was hard for him to sit still and quiet
all day when he'd already finished his work. After all,

he was only eight! He started to get in trouble for being fidgety. He got his name on the board for asking his neighbor a question.

Chris began to bring a book to school to pass the time. His love for science exploded as he read book after book. Unfortunately, even though his time was better spent, his behavior was still in question.

"Did you know that there are 150 different types of jellyfish in the Pacific Ocean alone?" he would excitedly ask his neighbor.

"Shhhhhh!" his teacher said, and on the board his name would go. Chris couldn't win.

Joan listened to this teacher complain about how Chris read in class. She couldn't help but giggle.

"What are you laughing at?" the teacher asked.

"The fact that you have a child who inhales books while most of us struggle with kids who couldn't care less."

Books are never a time waster; they are a time enhancer.

"When you are dealing with a child, keep your wits about you and sit on the floor."

—Austin O'Malley

Floor Show

Pamela disliked what she considered a teacher's uniform. It usually looked like some matronly dress or more often in an elementary setting it was a jumper or denim dress that was decorated with a variety of attention-grabbing paraphernalia. Button covers, I Love Teaching badges, and pins for every holiday and occasion. Pamela wore pants each and every day at her middle school. It was practical and even necessary. It's not that she faulted anyone else for the way they dressed, but a dress would just get in the way.

Sixth graders are a joy to teach. They are still young enough to get excited about learning but old enough to have the skills to produce quality work. Pamela knew it was a challenge to hold their attention at times, but she never ran out of ways to peak their curiosity. This was especially true right before Christmas break when all minds were somewhere else and not on the lesson at hand. Pamela launched one of her most reliable interest-seeking tools.

Amidst the chaos of students settling in after the bell had rung, students stumbled over something on the floor. It was Pamela! She was sitting right in the middle of the room peering into an opaque container, seemingly unaware of their stumblings. Moments later all the students were on the floor beside her quietly waiting for some explanation.

Pamela continued the lesson from the floor for the remainder of the class period. Her students' attention fixed and firm. It's a good thing she wore pants, huh?

Getting down to a student's level sometimes requires you to actually get down on the floor!

"The only reason I always try to meet
and know the parents better is because
it helps me to forgive their children."
—Louis Johannot

TK (Teacher's Kid)

Elizabeth wondered how long she should wait. It
had already been half the school year. She watched as
this fifth grader just barely got by. Being in the gifted
program brought with it certain expectations, and
this student wasn't meeting any of them. Elizabeth
knew that in these cases she was supposed to request
a reevaluation of the student to see if she still
belonged in the program. But Elizabeth was hesitant.
This child's mom was also a teacher of the gifted in
their district and well respected. She knew she'd be
starting a war if she proceeded. Still, she sent the
notice for reevaluation home.

Two days later, Mom, daughter, and the school's assistant principal showed up in her classroom for a meeting. Elizabeth was alone with her conviction. According to the assistant principal and the child's mother, Elizabeth's actions were unwarranted and unprofessional. Although Elizabeth's request for reevaluation was denied, she was glad that she had taken the risk of addressing the situation. Because of the meeting, Elizabeth discovered that the student had some health issues that were contributing to her lackluster performance in the classroom. The student's mom realized during their meeting that she should have shared that necessary piece of information with Elizabeth sooner.

While confronting this parent was anything but easy, Elizabeth felt good knowing that she had opened the lines of communication and would now be able to help this student succeed.

Having trouble with a teacher's kid (TK)? Remember to handle it with grace.

"Happy is the child who has wise parents
and guardians and whose training is
continued when he enters the schoolroom."
—Fanny Jackson Coppin

Perfect Match

Charlie was a teacher's kid now beginning kindergarten. He was already reading and knew how to do simple addition. His love for learning was insatiable and his temperament perfectionistic. His mother outlined to the principal his specific academic needs and requested a certain teacher. At first she was elated to find out that she got who she requested—until she walked her son to his class the first day.

The room was crowded and disorganized, even on the first day of school when teachers try to make their best impression on parents. Music blared from an unseen cassette player, and those children who had already arrived were either dancing wildly or coloring on the floor. Mom's shock must have been obvious because Mrs. Betts immediately approached her. Charlie, on the other hand, was desperately trying to pull from his mother's frightened grip to go play with the other children.

When he broke free, Mom tried to go after him muttering, "There's been a mistake!" Mrs. Betts led Mom to a table and said, "Your letter helped so much in determining the best placement for Charlie. In no time, you'll see him loosen up and learn to laugh at himself."

And she was right. Mom saw her son blossom socially, yet he retained his love for learning. In fact, it even flourished there. It was a good match after all.

> Every one of your students is a mother's child. Keep that utmost in your mind.

"Start a program for gifted children,
and every parent demands
that his child be enrolled."
—Thomas Bailey

Did He Pass?

Rob looked at his list of students to be tested and cringed—twenty-four kids to test in three days! Rob's testing was only the first step in a very long process to be placed in the school's gifted program. Only about 25 percent of those tested would actually qualify for the program. And many of those tested were referred by their own parents. Dealing with the disappointment and sometimes downright indignation of parents was the least favorite part of Rob's job.

Rob could usually tell within the first few minutes of testing whether or not a child would pass his screening test. It was obvious that this second grader wasn't going to make the cut. After testing he met with the parent privately and relayed the results. He could tell from her face. Rob thought to himself, *Another parent who is just convinced that her child is gifted.*

"Please, there must be some mistake," she said.

Rob responded with his all too familiar speech about how this test was not a full IQ test, only a screening instrument and that her son could take it again next year.

"You don't understand," the mom continued. "Mrs. Wickstrom is the best teacher here. She's our last chance to motivate Jon."

It's funny how parents flock to one program or another. It's not because they are elitist or because the program is the popular place to be. It's because a teacher has made it clear to all that kids are important.

A program is only as successful as its teacher.

"Let early education be a sort of amusement; you will then be better able to discover the child's natural bent."

—Plato

Stand at Attention

When Vanessa enrolled her five-year-old daughter, Kaitlin, in kindergarten she chose a private school. This school had a three-year waiting list, and Vanessa put Kaitlin on it when she was two. She was excited to finally be able to meet the teachers and tour the facility with the eyes of a kindergarten parent.

The rows of desks could not have been more perfectly aligned. Each prospective child's name was displayed on his or her future desk. The bulletin boards were color coordinated with each other, and the discipline plan was in plain sight in the front of the room. Each child had a construction paper bear with his or her name on it. Vanessa read the plan in horror.

Talking out of turn = take bear away

Moving out of seat = take bear away

Dropping pencil = take bear away

No homework = take bear away

Tardiness = take bear away

On and on it went. Vanessa's blood drained from her face as she asked, "But how do they get their bear back?"

The teacher looked at her in disgust. "Not until the next day when it starts all over again." This is the teacher Kaitlin would have in kindergarten? Vanessa politely thanked the teacher for her time and sprinted to the office to take Kaitlin off this hit list!

In discipline, break the will but preserve the spirit of a child.

117

> "The reward of a thing well
> done is to have done it."
> —Ralph Waldo Emerson

What Do You Deserve?

The disgruntled group of teachers left the retirement meeting disillusioned and disgusted.

"How can they do this to us? After thirty years of faithful service, I want what is coming to me." Cal Walsh had calculated his retirement benefits to the penny. He knew what he had coming to him, and now the district was telling him that there was no money! "I deserve that sick pay!" he ranted to no one in particular as he walked to his car.

The newspaper chronicled the grievances of both sides. Retiring teachers complained that they had been shafted. Administrators cited their contracts and reminded teachers that sick pay was a perk and not a right. It didn't change anything. There was no money. The bond issue had been rejected. Both sides were hurting. Both sides had forgotten why they were doing what they did.

Cal knew that money was not the reason he went into teaching in the first place. He remembered that, to him, it was his calling. Over time though, that calling had become a distant voice, barely audible.

Yes, the monetary rewards of teaching are few and far between. Will you finish well despite the lacking pay? Can you look back on your career year by year and know you gave your best? Can you recall the names and faces of those whose lives are changed because you were their teacher? Even if you can't, rest assured that they remember you.

Your value is measured by your legacy, not your salary.

> "Good discipline is a series of little victories
> in which a teacher, through small
> decencies, reaches a child's heart."
> —Haim Ginott

The Play's the Thing

Serena's attempt to fill in for the drama club leader was falling apart. She'd had no previous drama training, and even though she'd agreed to do this out of loyalty to her friend, she was regretting her decision. The students were unruly at best. They came to club unprepared, not knowing their lines. Serena knew her authority was being challenged and she needed to do something about it fast.

Two of the students who held the lead roles in the play were especially rude. In fact, they constantly harassed one student and brought her to tears on more than one occasion. Serena had warned them that if their behavior continued, she would pull them out of the play. She hoped her threat would never have to be carried out because opening night was in two weeks!

Again they showed up unprepared, and a tearful understudy fled the auditorium before rehearsal even began.

"You made the wrong choice," Serena scolded, and out they went.

Her drama coach friend called her that night furious that her best actors had been thrown out of the play. But Serena's decision stood, and she knew on opening night that it was the right one. The cast gave her a dozen roses presented by the formerly tearful understudy, who that night had the lead.

Make sure double standards never exist in your classroom. Wrong is wrong, no matter who commits it.

"Calming down a noisy, rebellious group of adolescents is a lot like defusing a bomb. Careful, premeditated, calm responses are crucial to success."
—James Nehring

Assignment Alma Mater

Eileen lingered at the locker, letting her fingers brush over the well-worn metallic numbers. Idly, she turned the combination lock and almost expected it to open. Of course it didn't—it hadn't been her locker in more than ten years! Looking down the all too familiar hallway, Eileen Dansk wondered if teaching at her old high school was such a good idea after all.

The first week of school brought with it even more nostalgic memories. Her homeroom buzzed about her presence and the fact that she still looked young enough to be in high school. It was then that she realized this wasn't a dream, but a reality that could easily overcome her. None of her students were in their seats, nor did it look as if they intended to sit down. Eileen stared at the pile of papers she was supposed to get these students to fill out. Her own experience in high school had not been all that pleasant. She'd never felt like she really belonged.

Her ninth graders didn't know that though, and Eileen capitalized on their ignorance. "I have thirty minutes to get you to fill out these forms. If you can do it in fifteen, then maybe I'll have time to tell you what it's going to take for you to really fit in at this school."

It's interesting how the promise of social

acceptance motivates kids to pay attention.

> Your own experiences in school can be used to improve those of your students.

"To learn to give up his own will to that of his parents or teacher, as we must to the Great Teacher of all, will surely make us happy in this life and in the life to come."

—Fanny Jackson Coppin

Are You Willing?

"I don't have to listen to you!"

"What will you give me if I do this?"

Karen's head was swimming with the voices of her indignant students. It was the first week of school, and she had already lost her grip on her eighth graders. But then she wondered if she ever had a hold of them in the first place.

Assignments had become bargaining sessions. If you do this, I'll do that. Finish this first, and then we'll do this. On and on it went, day after day. She wasn't teaching; she was begging! Karen remembered that when she was in school, she'd never dare argue with her teacher about the assignment. The teacher had the last word. But not anymore.

Yet she noticed that these same students never seemed happy or content. There was no joy in learning. There was negotiation in its place. Karen had played this game before and lost. It was time for a different strategy.

"I've got a deal for you," she began. "You work, and you'll pass. You don't work, and you'll fail."

Simple yet satisfying.

Break the will without crushing the spirit—that's great teaching.

"A problem is a chance for
you to do your best."
—Duke Ellington

Guess Who's Coming to Dinner?

Brenda watched the documentary about Japan with increasing interest as the reporters attempted to explain why Japanese students scored so much higher than American students on standardized tests. Three things jumped out at Brenda as being possible explanations. They had a longer school day and year. Teachers were highly paid and respected. Parents took major responsibility for their children's education and were very involved. Unfortunately, all these things were rarely found in the United States, if at all. "We are doomed!" Brenda said aloud.

One side note to the documentary captured Brenda's attention. It seems that teachers in Japan are required to visit the home of each of their students at least twice a month. Parents know that the teachers are there to check up on both the children and their parents. Brenda realized that this was one idea she could incorporate. *Parents and teachers always seem to meet on school turf,* she thought. *Why not meet on the family's turf?*

After calculating it out, Brenda figured she could visit three students per week. Her principal was impressed with her plan. It was the parents she needed to convince. After all, they were not used to a teacher making a social call. But how else could she really build a partnership with parents? The challenge was worth pursuing.

Work side by side with parents. Do whatever it takes to build that bridge.

"There is no shame in asking for help."
—William Glasser, M.D.

Prepare Ye

"How do you really prepare for your first teaching job?" Kal wondered aloud. He finally landed his first job with no time to spare. There were only two more days until pre-service. This was not how he had imagined it to be. He thought he'd be able to spend all summer gathering resources, working through the textbook, and lining up field trips and experts to visit his class. Instead, he barely had time to set up his grade book and number those textbooks.

Kal had the sinking feeling he would spend all year playing catch-up. And that's exactly what happened. He stayed barely one chapter ahead of his students. There was no time for him to plan field trips or devise any high interest activities. So he fell into assigning the chapters, collecting homework, and giving tests. This was not the kind of teacher Kal wanted to be.

For weeks he skipped lunch to stay ahead of the paper pile. One afternoon a colleague stopped by to ask if his class would be interested to join his on a field trip.

"It's last minute, I know. But Mr. Angler's class had to cancel and I need to fill the bus. It would really help me out if you'd come."

Kal's despair turned to relief as he realized the gift this teacher was offering him—a chance to break out of the box he had backed into.

Share your creativity and resources with others. You may be their answer to prayer.

"I had rather excel in knowledge
of what is good than in the extent
of my power and dominion."
—Alexander the Great

Boundary Breaker
by Tony Horning

When Dan Peters became a principal, he
eagerly anticipated breaking down the traditional
wall between the administration and faculty. After
many years in the classroom, he knew firsthand
the frustrations and hesitations of teachers. Dan's
goal was to create a nonthreatening, safe
environment—one that promoted community and
produced change. As he entered his office, he
determined to maintain an open door policy and
build meaningful relationships with his teachers.

Faculty meetings were his first opportunity to build those bridges. He brought new life to those meetings by encouraging participation. But he knew it would take time for his teachers to feel safe enough to take the risk and open their mouths. He also introduced a new process. Once a month, the teachers would meet as a group without him present. Once the meeting concluded, a representative would pass on anything requiring administrative input or action. This gave the teachers the chance to share concerns openly without fear that their supervisor would make a detrimental note about them.

Even though he had every right to be present, Dan chose to create a forum for teachers, new and veteran. He wanted his staff to know that he was more concerned with improving the school than with flexing his administrative muscles.

Have you thanked your principal lately, for the things he or she does to help make your job easier and more fulfilling? If not, make it your priority today.

"An error means a child needs
help, not a reprimand or ridicule
for doing something wrong."
—Marva Collins

Margin of Error

Group projects were always tiresome to
orchestrate, let alone grade. Someone always ended
up doing most of the work. Someone always
became disgruntled. And someone always slid by
doing nothing. Tensions rose and patience wore
thin as students tried desperately to work together,
something to which they were unaccustomed.

Barb had formed the groups herself this time.
They were quite diverse groups, each member with a
unique talent or strength. Each group had their own
topic to study and present to the class. Today was

presentation day. Barb had worked hard to comprise the groups to promote efficiency and quality. It was her decision that was also on the line today.

The first person in the group was designated as the speaker, the person who would present an overview of the project. Group One's speaker rattled off a five-minute overview of their project. When he was done, his group was speechless. The speaker had introduced the wrong topic. He was humiliated, and Barb was furious. How could he have made such a mistake? Barb had made sure each student knew his particular job in the group. They had worked for weeks on their parts.

Upon investigation, Barb realized that the mistake had been her own. She had taught them well how to do their parts. But she neglected to show them how those parts work together.

The next time a student makes a mistake, make sure that it's not your mistake you're seeing reflected instead.

"Why, then the world's mine oyster
Which I with sword will open."
—Shakespeare, *The Merry Wives of Windsor*

Freedom to Choose to Retire

by Helen Peterson

Anna qualified to retire with a good benefit package. However, she really didn't feel ready yet. When she asked herself what she'd rather be doing, the answer was always, "Nothing else." She felt much pleasure in teaching these young, eager students. Her principal and other teachers were her friends. Her life revolved around teaching.

Anna's dedication to her students continued, but new district and state testing made her question whether she was still teaching the way she wanted.

Finally, one fall, whenever Anna asked herself what else she'd rather be doing, she'd smiled and answered herself, "Join a writers' group, read, travel, work part-time in a bookstore, hike, bike, teach adults to read, volunteer in the soup kitchen, go for coffee with my husband, and maybe substitute every once in a while." The list kept growing.

She decided this was the year. She was young enough to enjoy so much more that life has to offer. But she decided to give herself a lifeline, that of renewing her teaching license one more time.

Don't be afraid to move on to another lifestyle when you feel the time is right. Don't feel guilty when you retire. Listen to that different drummer and bask in the freedom retirement gives.

> Retire when the timing is right for you. This is a personal decision.

"Stop talking so much. You never see a
heavy thinker with his mouth open."
—George Washington Carver

Lend An Ear

Tori couldn't believe it. She felt just as she had in
high school. She had been serious about school, but
many of the girls around her weren't. All they did
was chatter, especially while the teacher was talking.
They commented on so-and-so's outfit or hairstyle.
They made fun of those who weren't as popular or as
pretty. Tori had become annoyed at these girls who
got in the way of her actually learning something.
And now, during her first faculty meeting she was
experiencing the same frustration.

They were sitting right behind her and spoke in
just above whispers. Tori strained to block out their

voices to hear her principal. But the distraction was too great, and Tori found herself eavesdropping on their conversation. Believe it or not, they were critiquing the attire of each faculty member. Then they giggled at the bow tie the seventh grade science teacher wore. More high school horrors!

When the meeting ended, Tori nonchalantly turned to get a glimpse of the gossipers. They were picture perfect, dressed in the latest styles with perfectly manicured nails and flawless skin. Tori slipped out of the auditorium, praying that she would be unnoticed, and hid in her classroom.

You've got to be kidding! she thought. *No wonder we don't get treated like professionals; we're still in high school!*

Listen to yourself when you talk. You might be surprised at what you hear.

"Teaching, is not just a job. It is
a human service, and it must
be thought of as a mission."
—Dr. Ralph Tyler

Tell Me Why

(Written especially for the education
students at Keuka College, New York)

Amy was anxious to discover the tricks of her
trade. What works? What doesn't? Which
method, approach, or strategy would help make
her first year of teaching successful? Amy knew
that when learning something new, she should
ask someone experienced. So when a master
teacher visited her campus, she did just that.

"Why?" the teacher asked.

"What do you mean 'why'? Please tell me what
makes a successful teacher," Amy pressed.

"It's not the *who, what, where,* or even *how* questions that will get you your answer. Start by asking 'why.'

"As children, the question 'why' is most common and natural, yet we squash it. It makes grown-ups uncomfortable. 'Why' makes a person think— sometimes about things they don't want to think about. Yet in order to improve, in order to reach the unreachable, we must begin by asking 'why.'

"Why does Jane learn fast, yet John does not?

"Why isn't this math curriculum working?

"So the most important question isn't *how* I do what I do," the Teacher continued. "But '*why*' I do what I do."

Write it down, mull it over, but face it today and every day.

Each day ask yourself "why," and then you'll find out exactly what you need to do.

"Every job is a self-portrait of the person who does it. Autograph your work with excellence."

—Erik Erikson

50/50

"He's not pulling his weight around here!" Latisha finally complained aloud. She was tired of covering for Jim, tired of filling in the holes he left in their student's learning. This team teaching thing just wasn't working out. Math scores were considerably lower for all their students. Something had to be done, and Latisha was done doing it herself.

Sitting in her principal's office, Latisha listened as Mr. Balton tried to encourage her.

"I've known about Jim's weaknesses for quite some time," he confessed. "That's why I paired the two of you. I thought he'd learn from you since you are such a good teacher."

Latisha didn't know whether to be angry or thankful. He'd known all this time that Jim was weak in math?

"But I was wrong. First, forgive me for expecting you to do my job for me. It's up to me to make sure my teachers are getting the help they need. Second, don't give up on us, we'll work this out together."

"Well, I'm willing to do my part if you're willing to do yours. But what about Jim's part?" Latisha said.

"How about this instead? You give 100 percent and I'll give 100 percent. Part of mine is to mentor Jim. If we both give 100 percent, the students win!" Balton watched Latisha for signs of agreement.

After a long pause, Latisha finally smiled. "Yes, our students deserve all of me, not just part."

It was a good start.

Teaching is like a marriage. It's 100/100, not 50/50. Give it your all, regardless of what anyone else does.

"If you plan for a decade, plant a tree. If you plan for a century, teach the children."
—Anonymous

Arbor Day

Ms. Samuels' sixth grade earth science classes were involved in an extensive study of how plants affect their environment. An arborist, a horticulturist, and an environmentalist all came to speak to them about how they might have an impact on their local surroundings. Upon inspection of the school grounds, it was discovered that many of the trees were well over one hundred years old. As exciting as that was, it became quickly apparent that most of them were sick.

The dying trees posed several health and safety problems for the school. Huge infestations of insects lived in them; large limbs were threatening to fall;

and root systems were the culprits of uneven sidewalks. Ms. Samuels was proud of their discovery and presented their concerns to the local school board. Unfortunately, the school board didn't see the problem in the same desperate light they did.

I really thought this exercise would teach students how they could make their world a better place, Samuels thought. *All it did was teach them that it wasn't worth trying.*

The next week Ms. Samuels was called into the principal's office. The principal pointed to the morning's newspaper and asked, "Was this your doing?" The article featured ten of her students and their concerns for safety at the school due to the dying trees.

She smiled to herself, realizing that they learned a way to make a difference after all.

A lesson in real-life problem solving carries students into a promising future.

"Your children need your presence
more than your presents."
—Jean Kerr

Teacher Appreciation

The teacher's lounge began to fill with the aroma of various delectables. Sharon Mazer placed the bouquets of fresh flowers at each table. There were crisp, white linens, good china, polished silver, and even crystal goblets at each place setting. Classical music was piped in through the intercom system. Everything was perfect. Even the fluorescent lighting couldn't ruin the mood of this Teacher Appreciation Day.

Sharon and her makeshift crew of parents led the teachers to tables and began to serve them this lovingly prepared brunch. The teachers were overwhelmed by their kindness. Some even cried.

Sharon couldn't wait until the end of the brunch. She had something special planned.

As the brunch wound to a close, Sharon spoke eloquently about how teachers had touched her life as well as the lives of her children. "There is no greater calling," she said at the end. Then as if on cue, her servers approached each table with what seemed to be a bill in their hands. The teachers opened them with hesitance.

Ooh's and Ahh's exploded from the tables. The PTA had given each teacher a gift certificate to their favorite teacher supply store. The teachers were grateful, but Sharon only wished she could give them more. After all, how could she really repay people who had sacrificed so much just to teach.

Even if you've experienced only small doses of appreciation, know that the world couldn't progress the same without you.

"The real menace in dealing with a five-year-old is that in no time at all you begin to sound like a five-year-old."

—John Lubbock

Try It, You'll Like It

Sissy Randolph was grateful for a long-term substitute position in her neighborhood elementary school. Although she preferred older students, she looked forward to taking this kindergarten class for three weeks. How bad could it be?

After the fourth day, Sissy was ready to quit. She had no aide, and keeping up with twenty-five five-year-olds was the hardest job she'd ever had. She spent her day blowing noses, bandaging tiny fingers, tying endless pairs of shoes, and cleaning up from art time, snack time, and playtime.

Her only peace came during nap time, which was always too short. By the time she had convinced all of them to lie still and be quiet, there were only ten minutes left of that precious break. Sissy was convinced more than ever that she was not cut out to teach in the primary grades.

Sissy looked around at the room, much in need of a professional cleaning person. She couldn't leave the room this way. She wanted the regular teacher to come back to a clean, well-organized, and happy classroom. Just as Sissy was leaving, the real teacher returned. Amazed at what she saw, she thanked Sissy profusely as it was obvious she had left her class in capable hands.

Sissy couldn't get out of that room fast enough. *I want my mommy!* she thought as she raced out to the parking lot.

Find out which age you enjoy the most, then go and teach there.

"Some people succeed because they are destined to, but most people succeed because they are determined to."

—Austin O'Malley

Change of Plans

It's funny how teachers act like students whenever they get the opportunity, Betsy smiled to herself upon entering the year's first faculty meeting. They had a new principal, and it seemed that half the teachers were ready to give her a hard time and the other half were just silently hoping the life they enjoyed would not change. Betsy didn't like change, but maybe a new principal wasn't such a bad thing.

After polite introductions, the principal jumped right into changes to be made. "Some of us in teaching fly by the seat of our pants and hope that we eventually hit our targets and students will learn. But that rarely works, and I invite you to explore an alternative."

Betsy stared at the blank paper for the longest time, trying to figure out how to do such a foreign assignment. List at least three goals, professional, personal, and community-minded. Then make a plan of action to attain all three goals this year.

I've never thought about goals before! Betsy shuddered. *I don't even know how to begin.* And as if her principal read her thoughts she said, "Start by looking at relationships you'd like to improve, here, at home, with your students."

After some thought, Betsy decided her first goal would be to develop a positive relationship with her new principal.

How much effort do you put into your relationship with your principal? Remember that he or she is there to help you and needs your cooperation and support.

"A professional is someone who can do his best work when he doesn't feel like it."

—Diane Sawyer

Inclusion

"So what does inclusion include?" Dennis asked during a recent team meeting. The fifth grade teachers chose to give inclusion a try, although each had a different idea of how to go about it.

"My idea is that the special education teacher would float between our rooms all day as sort of a troubleshooter," one teacher explained.

"That's a good start," said another. "But it would be more helpful if I had her input as I plan lessons each week."

"True," said a third. "But wouldn't it be great if she could pull small groups to the side during instruction and make sure they 'get it'?"

The discussion went on like that for another hour, while Dennis just listened. New to this fifth grade team, he didn't want to make any waves. He had no experience in fifth grade. He had no experience with inclusion. And he didn't want to alienate his new team members, but he had a nagging question that he just couldn't shake.

"Excuse me," Dennis began. "These all sound like good ideas, and it is exciting to think of how they could impact our students, but I wonder . . ."

"What do you wonder?" one teacher asked with warning.

Dennis hesitated. "Two things. One, shouldn't we include the special education teacher in these discussions? After all, it's her job we're making decisions about. And two, what's our part here?"

Silence was the answer.

When talking about inclusion, be sure to include everyone who will be most affected by it.

"When one door of happiness closes,
another opens; but often we look so long
at the closed door that we do not see
the one which has opened for us."
—Alexander Graham Bell

Holiday Ho-Hum

Patricia's head was swimming with all the information she had acquired from both her diversity and sensitivity training. As a beginning teacher she was especially aware of doing a good job and meeting the needs of all her students, no matter how impossible it seemed. Yet all she could think about that day was how she would celebrate the coming holidays in her classroom.

Her own memories of holidays in school were special, and as a first grade teacher she couldn't imagine just ignoring them as her principal suggested. She stared at the blank bulletin board for what seemed like hours, unable to make up her mind. She didn't want to dictate any one holiday to her students.

"Well, I'm going to decorate it with things that make me feel good," she said and began cutting out construction paper decorations.

"What are you making?" an early arrival asked. But before Patricia could answer, the six-year-old began drawing decorations of her own.

Before the bell even rang, she was on the floor with ten children making holiday decorations for their bulletin board—each slightly different, each just as excited to make this bulletin board their bulletin board.

So Patricia didn't have to figure it out after all. The children had ideas of their own!

Involve students in the planning. It's one of the greatest motivators.

"You gain strength, courage, and confidence by every experience in which you really stop to look fear in the face. You must do the thing which you think you cannot do."
—Eleanor Roosevelt

Under Construction

The announcement was met briefly with applause, but only moments later turned into regret and concern. They all knew construction of the addition and remodeling of the existing buildings was well overdue, but the thought of teaching amidst the coming chaos was not inviting. Principal Lanning and his teachers were bracing for a difficult two years.

The cafeteria was the first to be relocated, and students had to eat in their classrooms. The teachers' workroom was next, and the copy machines and supplies were scattered throughout the remaining untouched areas. Tensions rose, parents complained that it was an unsuitable learning environment. Absenteeism on the parts of teachers and students rose.

Lanning, who still had five years left, seriously considered early retirement. But some teachers beat him to it, and those who remained looked to him for encouragement and leadership.

By the end of the first year of construction, parents had picked up the slack, and the morale in the school slowly improved. When the weather was good, they had picnic lunches outside, and Lanning reinstituted recess. And once a month the PTA dipped into their budget and provided a lavish catered lunch for the teachers. By the end of the construction, they were happy to have survived it, but they were also closer because of it.

A positive attitude is sometimes the only choice you have.

"Every great pitcher needs a great catcher."
—Casey Stengel

First Aide

Joan Steffand's new job as teacher's aide would be a welcome change. The school was within walking distance, and she would be working with a teacher that was well-respected. Days after being offered the job, she was in the classroom unpacking supplies from the summer. She had one concern. The last aide in this job had been with this teacher for fifteen years. How could this teacher come to depend on Joan as much as she depended on her last aide? Joan knew nothing of how this job worked.

"Hi. I'm Stacy Welch. And you must be my answer to prayer!" Stacy Welch immediately picked up a pair of scissors and joined Joan to cut out bulletin board decorations.

"Joan Steffand. Happy to be here," Joan eyed Stacy warily. Was she really at ease as she appeared?

Stacy could see that her new aide needed encouragement. "Joan, I'm so grateful you were available. The thought of beginning this school year alone was not a happy one."

"But you've taught this class for fifteen years. You don't really need an aide," Joan said.

"It's not a matter of ability, Joan. It's a matter of preference."

"But I'm only an aide," said Joan.

"This is our room, our students, and our job. Together we can make a difference," Stacy's resolve swept away any apprehension Joan had left.

Including others in your success is a vital part of creating an atmosphere of teamwork and cooperation in your classroom.

"You can work miracles by having faith in others. To get the best out of people, choose to think and believe the best about them."
—Bob Moawad

Fallen Angel

Cindy listened intently, surprised to hear that her friend had left her job as a school social worker to work in a hospital setting. "But Kendra, you seemed so happy at your first school. You told me you loved the people in the community and felt like you were making a real difference in their lives. What went wrong?"

Cindy had been Kendra's closest friend in college, and had shared Kendra's goal of becoming a school social worker. Confiding in her made Kendra feel better about her choice.

"After that school closed," began Kendra, "I had to take a job in a much larger district. I had to divide my time between five schools and wasn't able to form relationships with the students as before. My whole job description changed. It seemed like I was unofficially in charge of doing all the things no one else wanted to do. If a parent wouldn't sign certain placement papers, it was up to me to go confront them. If a student was physically disruptive in class, it was my job to contact the authorities.

"I started losing the love I once felt toward people. I felt myself becoming cynical and distrusting and began to forget why I'd become a social worker in the first place. I miss working with students, but my new job at the hospital is fulfilling, and I'm starting to feel needed and loved again."

Cindy was happy that Kendra had found a place where she could use her talents, but was saddened by the thought that the school system had lost such a caring person who could have been an integral part of helping students get a good education.

> Sometimes it's the unspoken expectations that drive good people away. Give everyone around you the support they desperately need.

"If you want help, help others. If you
want trust, trust others. If you want love,
give it away. If you want friends, be one.
If you want a great team, be a great
teammate. That's how it works."
—Dan Zadra

First Impressions

Sharon locked her car and walked slowly from
the school's parking lot to the front office. She
stopped midway, closed her eyes, breathed in the
crisp September morning air, and impressed the
memory. Her first day at her first teaching job—
Sharon, caught up in the moment, didn't see the curb
until it knocked her down, the contents of her new
soft-sided leather briefcase spilling onto the pavement.
Out of nowhere a hand reached down to her.

"First day?" Mike said helping Sharon to her feet.

"How could you tell?" Sharon joked to hide her embarrassment.

Once in the office, the secretary greeted her with a smile and a pile of supplies. She balanced her pile as she unlocked the door. Turning on the lights and closing the door, she surveyed the room—smaller than expected. She went to deposit her unwieldy pile and found no teacher desk. Now what? She would also need help carrying things in from her car. Eyeing the office call button, she hesitated. *What will they think of me? I need help already.* Before she could contemplate the answer, the intercom buzzed her instead.

"Miss Campbell, may I send a custodian down to help you set up your room?"

Sharon was speechless. She had been so worried about her own first impression. Look how marvelously this school had impressed her.

First impressions mean a lot. What impression have you made on your school today?

"Nothing great was ever
achieved without enthusiasm."
—Ralph Waldo Emerson

The Power of One

Being a mom, Wyn knew that her attitude and emotional state determined what kind of day she'd have with her family. If she was off, they were all off. What a terrible responsibility that is, to be a human barometer. Even with this knowledge, it took Wyn a lot longer to recognize how she affected her students as well.

There were days when, for one reason or another, she just didn't want to be there. There were days that she never stopped complaining. There were days that she couldn't smile, no matter how she tried. And on those days, her students' behavior mirrored her own. She believed their behavior was out of her control.

One day Wyn received notice that she received the grant she had worked all year on. It would supplement her classroom in a variety of ways. But most of all, it was an accomplishment that reenergized her attitude toward teaching.

In the weeks that followed she approached her job with a renewed sense of purpose and joy. Her students seemed to join in on her enthusiasm, and they, too, had a renewed sense of purpose. The funny thing is that Wyn had the power to change her students' behavior all along. The first step was to change her own.

Wondering why your class seems a little ho-hum? Try brightening your outlook, and see if it is reflected in your students.

"The more you love what you are doing,
the more successful it will be for you."
—Jerry Gillies

Homecoming

Christin cried as she walked out of her school for the last time. Yes, she'd miss the kids. Yes, she'd miss her friends. She'd even miss her mailbox! She knew the tears weren't logical, but they fell nevertheless. Her decision to stay home with her own children was applauded by some and criticized by others. And now as she walked to her car, all she could think about was what she was walking away from. Was it the right decision?

As the beginning of the next school year rolled around, Christin felt disconnected and disoriented. She had never not started school in the fall since before she was five. It didn't feel right. She began to daydream about what it would be like if she did go back. This life felt lonely. It was an unhappy first year at home.

Three years later, the beginning of the school year came and went without Christin even realizing it. She was so busy teaching preschoolers in her own home with her children that she didn't miss the school bell. Sitting with five four-year-olds on her living room floor was joyous.

At the end of one day, one of the moms from her little preschool paused at the door. "Christin, without your dedication, I don't think Jason would be ready for kindergarten next year. I just wanted to say thank you."

If home is where your heart is, go there and find out what work there is for you to do.

"Live your life so that your children can tell their children that you not only stood for something wonderful—you acted on it."
—Dan Zadra

Shining Star

Wolfgang Amadeus Mozart was a young musical genius. It was quite evident to his father from the very beginning that his son was uniquely talented. But he hesitated to teach him too early. He didn't want him to become disenchanted with music because he was pushed too soon. Yet when Mozart was four years old, Papa Mozart had no other choice but to teach his son himself. Already a gifted music teacher, Papa Mozart made his living as the court orchestra leader's assistant. He aspired to become the orchestra leader himself—the only job that would adequately support a family. But that was not to be.

Wolfgang's love for music and his desire to learn was insatiable. When most children groaned at the prospect of practicing for even an hour per day, Mozart had to be persuaded to stop practicing for at least some part of the day. By the age of five he was playing for audiences and bringing in much-needed money for his family. His father was compelled to give up his own dream in favor of his son's genius—the sacrifice of a loving father and teacher.

As teachers, we all choose to put our own aspirations aside for the next generation. Just as Leopold Mozart stepped aside so his son could shine, we must do the same.

Any glory a student attains falls naturally back on his teacher.

"Don't care what others think of what
you do; but care very much about
what you think of what you do."
—St. Frances DeSales

Honor Guard

Dan Shea paced up and down the aisles of his
tenth grade English class. It was the last day of their
standardized testing. Dan was tired, and he could
tell his students were as well. One in particular
could barely keep his head up. Dan knew that this
behavior meant a low score on the test. This was
one of his best students. He cringed at the thought
of the repercussions of a poor score on this test.

During their break, Dan consulted with his
colleague next door. His advice was not what Dan
had expected.

"Dan, you know the consequences if students do poorly on this test!"

"I know. I hate to think which class he'll be placed in next year," Dan said.

"No! It's not the kid I'm worried about. It's you!"

"Me?" Dan was confused.

"His failure is a blemish on your record. Do whatever it takes to prevent that, if you know what I mean."

Dan walked back to his room in shock. *Was he suggesting what I think he's suggesting?* Dan sorted the response forms from the test booklets. When he came upon his sleepy student's, he paused. He scribbled a note and attached it to the front of the form. The best he could do was inform the administration that the student was sleepy. Dan realized then that teachers are tempted to cheat for the same reasons students are.

Honor above all!

"One person can make a difference,
and every person should try."
—John F. Kennedy

A Seat of Honor

Sally Hill loved her job. Admittedly, teaching in a one-room schoolhouse had a myriad of challenges. They still existed in some black communities. It wasn't just the matter of teaching multiple grade levels or the inconveniences of such cramped surroundings that weighed on Sally's mind. It was the frustration of not being able to give her students all they would need to make it in this cruel world. And little Rosa, as smart as she was, lived with ridicule day in and day out.

Sally knew that showing favoritism toward students was not recommended, but if she could shelter and protect Rosa even just for those hours during the school day, she would feel like she accomplished something. One day the other kids teased Rosa mercilessly, and she began to cry. Sally motioned for Rosa to come up to her desk. From then on, she let Rosa sit up front with her whenever she felt sad.

Rosa Parks knew it was special to sit up front. And when she insisted on sitting up front in a bus in Montgomery, Alabama, she knew that it was wrong that somehow she wasn't considered special enough to sit there.

Sometimes special treatment is the kindest act of all.

"We must travel in the
direction of our fear."
—John Berryman

Leap of Faith

by Helen Peterson

Shirley and her husband had made long-range
plans. This was the year both had set for Shirley to
retire with good benefits.

Teaching had been a wise career choice for her.
Shirley had felt fortunate that she liked teaching,
even after that many years. She did have to admit,
however, that she'd felt more impatient the last
couple of years, but not as burned out as some
teachers she'd known.

Financially, she knew that she and her husband
had it together. She had aspirations and dreams
about next year when she retired.

But, still, she was apprehensive about really doing it. What if she missed teaching too much? What if she didn't have enough to do? What if? What if?

Then, she reviewed the feelings she always had when making major decisions and changes in her life through the years, and realized that basically she didn't like thinking about changes. But after they had happened, she had been satisfied with the outcomes.

As Shirley drove to the district office to hand in her resignation, she felt better. She knew that she wanted to make the leap of faith and retire.

Retirement is a major decision. Consider it well, but then trust that you've made the right decision.

Don't be fearful of change. Take that leap of faith.

> "Act as if what you do makes
> a difference. It does."
> —William James

Glittering Image

Donny Osmond, child star and teen heartthrob of the 1970's, thought he'd learned a lot about life as he and his siblings toured the world singing to millions of die-hard fans. After all, he had a tutor to make sure he was on track. He grew up in a large and loving family and was raised by parents he respected for their dedication, faith, and intelligence. He felt on top of the world until he was a grown man with his own family and life came crashing down.

Donny realized, much to his panic, that he knew very little about real life. He found out that even though he grew up in front of the whole world, he didn't know a thing about living in it. And now, as a father himself, he was determined that his own children would get a real education.

In his autobiography, Donny's concern about a quality education is evident. He says, "I wonder how many former child stars would say they got a great education." Donny missed out on all the social interaction of a traditional school experience. Even though he was always surrounded by people, his lessons were limited to how to "function in an adult world." How detrimental that was for Donny would become evident later in his life.

Sometimes we overlook the child when we focus on his talent. All children deserve a quality education, whether or not they are budding actors, singers, or sports stars.

Whether you're the teacher of a favorite or the famous, give them what they need— not your adoration, but a quality education.

"What will a child learn
sooner than a song?"
—Alexander Pope

The Sound of Music

The Sound of Music was Perry's favorite musical from childhood. As a music teacher, he reveled in its simplicity and grace. He loved music and loved children. His career choice was an easy one. But what of those children who had no talent nor the desire to immerse themselves in the magical world of music? The Von Trapp family singers are a legacy to many. But is it because of their devotion to music or their devotion to one another? Perry knew.

Perry made it a point to meet with teachers from every grade level over the summer. What were they learning that he could put to music and therefore make it easier for all of them to learn?

"After all, we all learned our ABC's that way," Perry explained during one such meeting. By the time school started, he had written songs to teach the states and their capitals, the continents and the oceans, the presidents, the prepositions, and even the categories of animals.

The point of his effort was not to produce a concert of his original songs. It was not to attract publicity to his ever vulnerable music program. It wasn't even to entice students to take up a musical instrument. The end result Perry hoped for, and ultimately found, was that there would be joy in the journey—that the music would move the minds and the hearts of his students.

Use your own passion to ignite the passion inside your students.

"We loved the doctrine
for the teacher's sake."
—Daniel Defoe

The Testing

(Dedicated to the students in the education
department at Clearwater Christian College)

The first time is always the hardest. It's always
the most consuming. And it's always the most sweet.
Teaching future teachers was the most rewarding
work Vikki had ever done. It had a definite domino
effect, reaching far into the future. She laughed
aloud as she remembered her own reaction to this
teaching assignment. *Assessment!* How could she
possibly make such a dry topic come alive?

Twenty-five college juniors and seniors in the
education department of a small private college
had gathered with a collective groan. This was a

dreaded class—one avoided until the very end when students had run out of all other options. All they knew was that it was boring but necessary and definitely hard. Vikki remembered when she herself had taken this same class. It was indeed all they feared. But she didn't want to see fear in their faces each week. She wanted to see intrigue and delight.

She brought them out of their comfort zones of reading, listening to lectures, and taking quizzes and expected of them professional standards, insights, and discussion. She modeled for them what she expected, and they rose to the occasion. The workload was heavy; but the support was strong, and victory was won! Students left her class equipped and motivated. Vikki collapsed with sweet exhaustion when the semester was through. Now she watched as each of

their lives touched hundreds more.

When you have a chance to teach teachers, give them what you expect them to pass on to their students.

"From the very beginning of his
education, the child should
experience the joy of discovery."
—Alfred North Whitehead

Dream Weaver

Mr. Crites was skeptical of his newest student,
Neil. Although he was new to this high school as
well, he questioned the advanced placement of any
student. Most of these students were pushed hard by
their parents into situations they were just not ready
for. Pride in their children's accomplishments drove
parents to skip them one and sometimes two grades
ahead. And Neil's records indicated this same pattern.

"We moved here especially because of Blume
High School's reputation in the sciences. Neil is
both talented and driven," Mrs. Armstrong

explained during their conference. Mr. Crites wasn't surprised. Most parents said the same thing.

But Neil surpassed everyone's expectations, even Mr. Crites'. In fact, Mr. Crites became caught up in Neil's drive to prepare for the life he dreamed of. They began to spend every afternoon together in the science lab discovering how the world worked.

Neil Armstrong's dream might not have been realized if it were not for teachers who could see how a dream could be turned into reality.

Forgotten how to dream? Start by dreaming the dreams of your students.

"If you can learn from hard knocks,
you can also learn from soft touches."
—Carolyn Kenmore

Power Up

Brad was warned before he took his first
teaching job that those who have the real power in
a school may not be who one would expect. The
principal's secretary, definitely. The head custodian,
most often. The cafeteria manager, many times. But
Brad wasn't at all prepared for who had the power
in his school—not until it was too late.

At first he couldn't figure out why, after
following the directions in his orientation packet,
his copies had not been run. Again and again he
found them off to the side, out of the pile. He also
noticed that his name was misspelled on his
mailbox. By the end of the second week, he figured

that somehow he was missing some important nugget of information. The workroom aide always seemed incredibly busy, and he didn't want to bother her. But he just needed to know why his stuff wasn't getting done.

The conversation lasted only seconds. This aide had a major attitude problem, one that he seemed to somehow aggravate. An hour later he was called into his principal's office, and there sat the workroom aide with a sly smile on her face. Brad was reprimanded for both not following procedure and antagonizing the aide. He was dumbfounded and speechless.

There were rules here. Rules that a person didn't know about until he had broken them. And the workroom aide was the enforcer.

Brad chose to do his own copying for the rest of the year.

Give new teachers the inside scoop, just as you wish someone had for you.

"We shouldn't teach great books,
we should teach a love of reading."
—Burrbus Frederic Skinner

Just Too Much

The training for this new reading program was grueling. Eve hoped it would be worth it. It involved so much more on the teacher's part for both preparation and instruction. It was definitely not the status quo. Yet, at the same time, it was exciting to break out of the mold. It could ignite a love for the classics she has never before witnessed in students or teachers. But she could tell that her colleague, who also took the training, was not as convinced. It was just too much work.

Eve worked hard to secure the funds necessary for this program in her middle school. In order for the program to accomplish its objectives, it had to be used as prescribed in training. After six weeks Eve was exhausted, but her students were on fire for the classics. Their enthusiasm was enough to keep her going. By the end of the year, she was confident that the program would receive rave reviews from parents, students, and administrators, ensuring future funding.

But the surveys came back unexpectedly negative. Eve couldn't believe that half of the students didn't feel the program was any different than anything else. Half—how could that be? During a meeting with her principal, she found out. The students taught by her colleague were the dissatisfied customers. She refused to implement the program as prescribed. "Just too much work," she admitted finally. And so a dream ended.

Are you a dream maker or a dream breaker?

"The world is all gates, all opportunities,
strings of tension waiting to be struck."
—Ralph Waldo Emerson

Judge Not
by Helen Peterson

Beth had just accepted a full-time teaching position at another school in the district, starting the following fall. Since her current assignment was a temporary contract, she was grateful and excited for the chance to have her own class. She was going to miss the friendships of teachers, the principal, students, and parents here at this school, but she was ready to take on the responsibility and commitment to the new school.

Much to her dismay, when she announced her news in the teachers' lounge, some of the veteran teachers were not elated for her. Instead, they recounted the negative experiences they had teaching at that school. They told her she wasn't going to like it there.

Beth listened quietly to their laments, but in her heart she decided she was going to love teaching at that school. She was going to find the teachers and principal interesting and supportive. She was going to appreciate the uniqueness of each student and teach them well. And you know what? She did!

Being happy and content is a state of mind. Look for the positive in every new change. Don't take the negative from others and assume it's all true. Bonding to a new environment is a challenge that needs to be met. Don't let others' opinions spoil it.

Search for the positive experiences in your journey, and you'll find them.

"Those having torches will
pass them on to others."
—Plato

An Olympic Moment

As chairman for the Special Olympics in her district, Laura Burns did everything she could to include as many students as possible in the games each year. The more the competition, the better the athletes would be who would rise to the top. As a marathon runner herself, Laura knew the pleasure and satisfaction attached to competing in a challenging event. Then an unexpected honor presented itself to Laura and her district.

With more than a hundred students from her district competing in Special Olympics, carrying the torch from one point to another was especially challenging. How could she include all her students in this special honor? As a runner, Laura was asked to do the actual running, and her students could watch. But to Laura, that wasn't good enough.

The day came, and everyone squinted as they watched the horizon for the runner who would pass the torch to Laura. "There he is!" someone shouted and a roar of cheers went up from the gathering crowd. Laura was ready for the handoff.

As the runner neared her position, Laura began running along in a line with her one hundred students ahead of her. When the torch was passed successfully, Laura took that split second to sense the warmth of the flame and closed her eyes in thanksgiving. Then she passed the torch on to the student closest to her, who ran ahead to the next runner.

You've prepared them well. Know when it's time to pass the torch.

"The art of teaching is the
art of assisting discovery."
—Mark Van Doren

With the Greatest of Ease

Fa•cil•i•ta•tor - n. One who makes things easy or less difficult.

Gwen stared at the overhead and wondered, *Am I a facilitator?* The workshop just seemed more of the same until this issue was introduced. And now she was really wondering about herself. She taught advanced classes, and her students always seemed to be struggling. Her intent had never been to make it easy for them—actually just the opposite.

She thought back over her teaching style. Overheads, lecture formats, note taking for students, use of textbooks and other resource materials—all of it was standard issue in teaching. But did it all "make things easy or less difficult" for her students? Gwen doubted it.

For some reason, she couldn't go back to business as usual at school. This workshop had really gotten under her skin. Finally, out of desperation and hoping for some peace of mind, she did what any good teacher would do. She looked it up: *Facilitate.*

She learned that it means to accelerate, advance, enable, promote, and serve and that it doesn't mean to complicate, discourage, hinder, or obstruct.

Gwen's shoulders slumped, and her head fell. She had wanted to challenge her students, but she realized at that moment that she hadn't been giving them the tools they needed to meet the challenge. That was the day Gwen switched sides.

Which side are you on?

"My idea of education is to
unsettle the minds of the young
and inflame their intellects."
—Robert Maynard Hutchins

At the Movies

Syd left the movie theater amazed that again a
film had been made that touched him deeply
because it was about teachers and teaching. It wasn't
the first time. He thought back over all the films he
had seen in recent years that touched on the
resiliency of the human spirit in teachers—how it
somehow defies the odds and inspires students to
great heights. This film, *Mr. Holland's Opus*, was a
little different. Its focus was on the teacher himself
and his struggles with the fact that he was a teacher
at all. In a society that often doesn't value the

importance of teachers, this film sent a reminder that we need not depend on the approval and accolades of others to validate why we do what we do.

Syd had a hard time accepting the fact that he was a teacher himself. After years in a mismatched career, he took a leap of faith and went into teaching. Against his will, he stepped into this brave new world called school. It took taking himself out of his comfort zone to see the possibilities for himself and students. The realization that this life was a gift was hard to explain to anyone else but another teacher. Syd knew the only course of action was to pass on the torch to his students. That way they, too, could receive this gift and inspire others along the way.

It may seem corny to cry at movies about teachers and teaching. But you won't be crying alone in that theater.

> Passing the torch to your students means setting them on fire for life.

"Good teaching is one-fourth
preparation and three-fourths theater."
—Gail Godwin

Sight Unseen

Mandy eyed the room full of fifth graders and
desperately wished she were somewhere else,
anywhere else! Then to add to her apprehension
she caught her reflection in the glass doors and
cringed at her lack of hair, hollow eyes, and less
than rosy complexion. The chemotherapy had
done its job. The cancer was gone, but the calling
card it left was hard to ignore. What would the
children think? All they would do is stare at her.
They'd never hear the story.

The library was abuzz as the students watched
Mandy walk onto their makeshift stage. She settled
into the chair and unpacked her guitar. Mandy was

sure she heard muffled giggles from the back. She knew that it wouldn't be long until she had their attention, but for the wrong reasons.

After ten minutes of musical storytelling and quick changes, Mandy looked just briefly into the eyes of a girl in the first row. Those eyes were laughing. But it wasn't her patchy hair or the dark circles under her eyes that made her smile. It was the escapades of Scooby-Doo that Mandy spun with her guitar. At the day's end, she was surrounded by students and their questions. But they weren't the kinds of questions Mandy expected. "How do you make your guitar sound like a truck?" Relief flooded Mandy as she realized that they had seen her after all—the real Mandy, not the shell.

Good storytelling is a lost art. It distracts the mind from what is seen and draws it into only what can be imagined.

"At every step a child should be allowed to meet the real experiences of life; the thorns should never be plucked from his roses."

—Ellen Kay

To Read or Not to Read

Tamara tossed and turned all night before finally settling with herself that she would indeed present a certain story to her sixth graders that next day. She knew it was risky. She knew someone might complain. But the value of the story overrode her hesitancy. After all, the classics were the classics, whether a character dies in them or not.

The students were mesmerized as Tamara read aloud. She loved reading aloud, and it showed. At the climax of the story, the main character, a kid their age, died. Everything in the story pointed to that probability, but the students were still caught off guard. A class discussion ensued, and Tamara was so pleased to see that they were really thinking the story through. Their conversations continued well after they left class. And that's when the phone started to ring.

"How could you expose my child to death?"

"How could you read a story where a child dies?"

As Tamara sat in her principal's office, she heard her on the phone with a complaining parent. "Ms. Simpson is one of my best. I have no need to censor her."

Did Tamara regret reading that classic to her students? No. Did her principal regret her reading it? No. Did her students regret her reading it? Not at all. And if it started conversations in their homes about what they did in school, it was worth it!

Your decisions may not always be popular. Just make sure your reasons for them can stand alone.

"We teach more by what we
are than by what we teach."
—Will Durant

Smiley

Mr. Cross ran a tight ship. It was obvious he believed fear to be a great motivator. He tolerated no frivolity and no smiling. Not only did he never smile, he discouraged smiling in students as well. Samuel Clemmens just couldn't stand school because of no smiling. Wasn't life supposed to be fun?

The days were long and tedious. Sam just couldn't keep his lessons in his head. While daydreaming one day, he wondered, *Why is Mr. Cross so cross?* A sly smile graced his face for an instant. In his best handwriting, he wrote an appropriate rhyme about Mr. Cross on his slate, which he easily slid to his neighbor. Within minutes, giggles filled the air, and Mr. Cross's happiness antennae went up in a fury. Scanning the classroom for the culprit, he noticed that Sam was the only one looking seriously at his arithmetic. Curious?

Mr. Cross was the topic of Sam's poetry, the beginning of a distinguished writing career. One never knows how the imagination of his students will be triggered.

There's a chance you will become a character in your student's life story. Are you the good guy or the bad guy?

"There is nothing in a caterpillar that
tells you it's going to be a butterfly."
—William H. Danforth

The Daily News

Glen surveyed his senior journalism class. It
had been a long and challenging year. So many of
these students had been with him since their
freshman year. He remembered their first days
together as if it were yesterday. They could barely
put complete sentences together, let alone
independently run the school's newspaper. He
thought that by the end of high school, they would
be professionals. But for some reason Glen was still
waiting—waiting for these seventeen- and
eighteen-year-olds to act like professionals.

No one seemed to be able to concentrate on
this last issue. Their minds were filled instead with

signing their annuals, summer plans, and summer loves. Glen felt like he was putting this issue together by himself. That's not what he had trained them to do. They had everything they needed to make it in the real world—or did they?

Two years later Glen ritualistically flipped through his morning paper. His eyes fell on the editorial page where a new columnist held the prized spot. He squinted his eyes to be sure he was seeing right. There in front of him was the byline of one of his students. The title of his column was, "Those Who Give Us Wings." The carefully crafted story was about an old journalism teacher who had given this author his wings.

Be patient.
Even a
butterfly
can't fly until
his wings dry.

"People seldom see the halting and painful steps by which the most insignificant success is achieved."
—Annie Sullivan

Little by Little

Cheri watched closely as the aide fed Michelle. It was always the same—first the positioning of Michelle in the chair and strapping her in, then the bib, then the introduction to the food placed in front of her. Janice, the aide, reminded Michelle at each mealtime what time of day it was, what she was eating, and what she would do with the fork or spoon. It was a painstakingly slow process, yet Janice was always full of encouragement and patience, something Cheri had been lacking lately.

Her intermediate varying exceptionality class may have been small in comparison to a regular fourth grade classroom, but the demands were infinitely greater. Cheri had been teaching it for ten years, and she could feel burnout right around the corner. Many of her colleagues had already left this kind of classroom. They were always amazed to hear that Cheri was still at it. They weren't the only ones who wondered why.

"I see so little progress," she said to her husband. "I think this will be my last year."

Her principal was not happy with Cheri's news that she wanted to transfer. He knew how difficult it was to integrate a new teacher into this kind of situation.

On her last day, Cheri fed Michelle herself. As she lifted the spoon to her lips, she saw it! A smile! "Did you see that?"

"Yes," said Janice. "And it was all for you."

Cheri rescinded her resignation.

Sometimes just the simplest of steps are enough to encourage us to continue.

The mediocre teacher tells.
The good teacher
explains.
The superior teacher
demonstrates.
The great teacher
inspires.

—William Arthur Ward

About the Author

A veteran educator and curriculum designer and author of the best-selling book *Apples and Chalkdust,* **Vicki Caruana** loves to encourage teachers! She is frequently a featured speaker at conferences for educators, homeschoolers, and parents. Presently she spends most of her time writing for a wide variety of publications, including *ParentLife, Parenting for High Potential,* and *Discipleship Journal.*

She credits her inspiration to her first grade teacher, Mrs. Robinson at Mount Vernon Elementary School, who influenced her decision at age six to become a teacher, and to her family with whom she now lives in Colorado Springs, Colorado.

For additional information on seminars, consulting services, to schedule speaking engagements, or to write the author, please address your correspondence to:

vcaruana@aol.com

Additional copies of this book
and other books by Vicki Caruana
are available from your local bookstore.

Apples & Chalkdust
Apples & Chalkdust (gift edition)

If you have enjoyed this book, or if it has impacted
your life, we would like to hear from you.

Please contact us at:

RiverOak Publishing

Department E

P. O. Box 700143

Tulsa, Oklahoma 74170-0143

www.riveroakpublishing.com